A TREASURY OF
IBN TAYMIYYAH

THE TREASURY SERIES IN
ISLAMIC THOUGHT AND CIVILIZATION

Mustapha Sheikh

❧ ❧ ❧

كنوز من ابن تيمية

A Treasury of
Ibn Taymiyyah

*His Timeless Thought
and Wisdom*

KUBE
PUBLISHING

TO MY PARENTS

رَّبِّ ارْحَمْهُمَا كَمَا رَبَّيَانِي صَغِيرًا

*A Treasury of Ibn Taymiyyah: His Timeless
Thought and Wisdom*

First published in England by
Kube Publishing Ltd
Markfield Conference Centre
Ratby Lane, Markfield
Leicestershire LE67 9SY
United Kingdom

TEL +44 (0)1530 249230
FAX +44 (0)1530 249656
WEBSITE www.kubepublishing.com
EMAIL info@kubepublishing.com

CIP data for this book is available from the British Library.

ISBN 978-1-84774-103-5 casebound
ISBN 978-1-84774-106-6 ebook

Cover design Inspiral Design
Book design Imtiaze Ahmed
Arabic & English typesetting nqaddoura@hotmail.com
Printed by Mega Basim, Turkey

Contents

Transliteration Table

Arabic Consonants

Initial, unexpressed medial and final: ء ʾ

ا	a	د	d	ض	ḍ	ك	k
ب	b	ذ	dh	ط	ṭ	ل	l
ت	t	ر	r	ظ	ẓ	م	m
ث	th	ز	z	ع	ʿ	ن	n
ج	j	س	s	غ	gh	هـ	h
ح	ḥ	ش	sh	ف	f	و	w
خ	kh	ص	ṣ	ق	q	ي	y

with a *shaddah*, both medial and final consonants are doubled.

Vowels, diphthongs, etc.

Short: ◌َ a   ◌ِ i   ◌ُ u

Long: ◌َا ā   ◌ِي ī   ◌ُو ū

Diphthongs: ◌َوْ aw

                ◌َيْ ay

Acknowledgments

I would like to thank my dear friend and colleague, Tajul Islam, for contributing his thoughts on *takfir* that form the basis of Chapter 18. Usaama al-Azami's editorial support has been invaluable throughout the publication process, and he has often gone beyond the call of duty—I pray Allah reward him for his efforts. I am grateful to Yahya Birt for coming up with the original idea for a book on Ibn Taymiyyah and for suggesting me as its author. Finally, my gratitude to my wife, Sofia Rehman, for reading the final version and providing very useful suggestions for its improvement.

Introduction

haykh al-Islām Ibn Taymiyyah is doubtless the most famous and, in many ways, the single-most important intellectual figure in all of Mamluk history. Born in Ḥarrān on 22 January 1263 to a family of Ḥanbalī *ulama*, he and his family were forced to flee their home as a result of the Mongol invasions. In a near escape, the family was able to reach Damascus safely, where they subsequently took up permanent residence. *Shaykh al-Islām*'s early years were spent in study, firstly with his father, and then with a number of prominent Ḥanbalī *ulama* of Damascus. Theology, Sufism, logic, philosophy and heresiography were subjects which he gained quick mastery over, besides the foundational disciplines typical of any scholar's education, such as Hadith, *fiqh* and the memorisation of the Qur'an. He quickly demonstrated unique intellectual prowess, which led to his appointment as mufti at the tender age of seventeen. By twenty-five, he had succeeded his father in the capacity of *shaykh al-ḥadīth* at the Sukkariyyah school in Damascus and was appointed to a chair in the Umayyad mosque for the teaching of exegesis.

In the following years, Ibn Taymiyyah would have endless encounters with the authorities and rival *ulama*, and endure imprisonment on no less than six separate occasions between 693/1294 and 728/1328. The official stance of the authorities was that his teaching had to be restricted since he was propagating doctrines which threatened the salvation of individual Muslims and the stability of the regime, such that the Sultan, as defender of the order, had to take appropriate action. The reality was quite different, and involved a complex of several factors: the political capacity of the *ulama* as advisers to the Mamluk emirs; the rivalry among the *ulama* to fill this function; the tendency toward doctrinal uniformity as a means of increasing the power of the *ulama*; the growing power of the Sufi orders; and the popularity which *Shaykh al-Islām* enjoyed with the masses.[1] It would seem that *Shaykh al-Islām*'s fortunes, quite soon after his initial prominence, had taken a turn for the worse. He, however, interpreted the events that befell him in life quite differently. Famously, he responseded to the trials he endured, as confided to his closest student, Ibn Qayyim al-Jawziyyah, with the following word: 'Paradise is in my heart—wherever I go, it remains with me. My imprisonment is spiritual retreat; my execution is martyrdom; my being exiled from my land is emigration.'[2]

In spite of the efforts of the authorities to circumscribe his influence, Ibn Taymiyyah succeeded

---

1. D. Little, 'The Historical and Historiographical Significance of the Detention of Ibn Taymiyya', *International Journal of Middle East Studies* (4) 1973, pp. 311-327, p. 326.

2. See Chapter 10 for commentary on this statement.

in creating a legacy unparalleled in the world of classical Muslim thought, one which would impress on all branches of learning and scholarship. The occasions in prison when he was prevented access to books thwarted him not in the least. He simply relied on his infallible memory and continued to write lengthy treatises and responsa in the service of his followers.

Today, nearly seven-hundred years after his death in a prison in Damascus in 728/1328, *Shaykh al-Islām* Ibn Taymiyyah remains one of the most intriguing of the classical Islamicate thinkers. This is because, despite the breadth and depth of his intellectual legacy, he is more often than not identified as the intellectual forebear of contemporary Islamic radicalism and militancy, especially since 11th September 2001. In the words of Yahya Michot, 'Whether coming from government circles or militant Islamists, from incompetent Orientalists or the Western media, a plethora of writings accuse Ibn Taymiyyah of opposition to reason, mysticism, of fundamentalism and intolerance, of radical extremism.'[3] No doubt the frequent references to *Shaykh al-Islām*'s fatwas in the writings of modern jihadi ideologues has only bolstered the image of him as the spiritual father of modern Muslim extremism. Much earlier than 11 September 2001, his name was

---

3. Y. Michot, *Ibn Taymiyya: Against Extremisms* (Paris: Editions Albouraq, 2012) p. xx.

already implicated in the assassination of Anwar Sadat in 1982. The assassin, Khalid Islambuli, who proclaimed moments after the operation that he had killed the Pharaoh, had been inspired by texts which were based on the anti-Mongol fatwas, in which Ibn Taymiyyah had reasoned that the Mongols of Iran were unbelievers because they did not rule by the Shariah. And more recently, we are beginning to learn of the centrality of Ibn Taymiyyah for the ideological outlook espoused by ISIS. *The Guardian* quoted an ISIS fighter, Abu Moussa, in January 2015: 'People say al-Dawla ['The Islamic State'] excommunicates Muslims; we don't do that. Yes, we have no tolerance for anybody who opposes our message. Why do we fight the Free Syrian Army? We spread our message by proselytisation and sword. Ibn Taymiyyah said, "The foundation of this religion is a book that guides and a sword that brings victory."'[4] These are three examples—many more could be given.

Yet it is also abundantly clear from Ibn Taymiyyah's magnificent corpus that there is more to his work than simply pro-jihad fatwas—and much, much more than *Islam for Dummies* would have us believe. In this context, this short book seeks to present a fresh reading of *Shaykh al-Islām*, one which exhibits his penetrative insight and timeless

---

4. Hassan Hassan, 'The secret world of Isis training camps – ruled by sacred texts and the sword', *The Guardian*, 25 Jan. 2015, https://www.theguardian.com/world/2015/jan/25/inside-isis-training-camps (accessed 28 Sep. 2016).

wisdom. In essence, it aims to recast him for a new generation of Muslims who are seeking a pathway through the challenges of the modern age. To some, Ibn Taymiyyah could not possibly serve this purpose; I would contend that there is no scholar of the classical age of Islam better suited than he for this. In the words of Professor Yahya Michot, the leading expert on Taymiyyan thought: 'As for the ideas that the *Shaykh al-Islām* himself expresses in his multiple writings, far from being simplistic thinking that the ignorant attribute to him, they have never had a greater present resonance. Rather than belonging in a museum of medieval thought—or the monopoly of ISIS militants—they have, truly, the timelessness of the great Muslim tradition. May they, as God wills, have enlightened not just one spring, but inspire many more in the future, for the greater glory of God, the happiness of the Muslims and the well-being of mankind.'[5] With raised hands turned upwards towards the Heavens, we have only to say, *amīn*!

---

5. *Ibn Taymiyya: Against Extremisms*, p. XXIX.

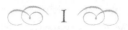

Names

فَلَا تَعْدِلُ عَنِ الْأَسْمَاءِ الَّتِي سَمَّانَا اللهُ بِهَا إِلَى أَسْمَاءٍ أَحْدَثَهَا
قَوْمٌ - وَسَمَّوْهَا هُمْ وَآبَاؤُهُمْ - مَا أَنْزَلَ اللهُ بِهَا مِنْ سُلْطَانٍ.

Let us not turn ourselves away from the names with
which God has named us for the names that some people
have invented, that they have given, they and their
fathers, and for which God never sent down any
enabling authority.[6]

*T*he act of naming has a force all of its own. While
it has the power to elevate, it also has the power to
debase. Names convey symbolic ideas beyond their
meaning. They have the power to set a person upon
a path destined for greatness, yet they also have the
power to ruin a person, rendering life a misery. As
one writer has put it, the power of names is 'like an

---

6. *Ibn Taymiyya: Against Extremisms*, pp. 20-21.

invisible pressure which intercepts our thoughts and actions, distorts beyond recognition the mirror and makes us vulnerable to the pain of the past and the fear of the future.'[7] Such power is usually associated with God alone, and so the intrinsic power of the act of naming is in some way an affront to God, inasmuch as it is a source of power besides God—it is in some sense a pathway to associationism, *shirk*, from this particular angle. Naming also draws lines, divides, dichotomises, bifurcates, establishes an 'us' and a 'them', and can lead therefore to any number of problematic outcomes. Naming when used for the purposes of categorisation can lead to a better understanding of the world—to knowledge—but it can also bring about ignorance in all of its forms—intolerance, bigotry, prejudice, chauvinism, even despotism. Herein lies the root of the issue highlighted by *Shaykh al-Islām* Ibn Taymiyyah. Whereas names invented by man have both the potential for goodness and evil, names that God has chosen for us are purely good. They are a cause for unity rather than division; they are a representation of the reality of things rather than their accidental qualities. *Shaykh al-Islām* warns against the great harm that the act of naming can do to a community, especially in terms of creating division. Baseless names for which God has never sent any enabling authority—names which are not to be found in God's

---

7. M. Beron, *The Power of Labels* (Indiana: AuthorHouse, 2013), p. ix.

revelation or in the teachings of His final Messenger. When a Muslim is asked who he is, he should not say that he is this or that; he should say that he is a Muslim; this is in adherence to God's Book and the Sunnah of His Messenger. Yet at the same time, no one has the right to put to trial those who have chosen for themselves names that are permitted to them, such as may be associated with an imam, or a shaykh or a school of thought. Whether then someone chooses the self-appellation Ḥanafī, Shāfiʿī, Mālikī, Jaʿfarī or Ḥanbalī; or indeed Sunni, Shiʿi, Ṣūfi or Salafi; or even Traditionalist, Modernist, Feminist or Agnostic—whatever the name, 'there shall be no friendship on account of these names, nor hostility on the basis thereof. On the contrary, the most noble of creatures in the sight of God is the one among them, of any group whatever, who most fears Him.'[8] And God knows best!

---

8. *Ibn Taymiyya: Against Extremisms*, p. 22.

2

Paradise

إِنَّ فِي الدُّنْيَا جَنَّةً مَنْ لَمْ يَدْخُلْهَا لَا يَدْخُلْ جَنَّةَ الآخِرَةِ.

In this world there is a paradise. Whoever does
not experience it, will not experience the Paradise
of the Hereafter.[9]

---

*I*n Paradise there is only peace, prosperity and
happiness. For some, the very thought of this will
contrast starkly with their experience of this world.
Experience of the harsh reality of the world may
even make any attempt to conceive such a state
very difficult. And while the fundamental nature
of the world we inhabit has changed little through
time—inasmuch as good and evil continue to be
omnipresent—our engagement with and perception
of the world, and our perception of our own place
within it, has surely evolved with the onset of

---

9. *Al-Wābil al-ṣayyib*, p. 109.

modernity. Many of us, despite possessing the means to sustain a largely comfortable existence, compare ourselves to others which can leave us feeling that we are not good enough, do not have enough, are not doing enough, and so on. Anxiety, panic and depression are too often the resultant conditions, and they are on the rise. It is now a fact that one in three of us will at some point in life suffer from one or another mental health issue. In light of this, the words of *Shaykh al-Islām* Ibn Taymiyyah take on a new hue of meaning; they are a reminder and encouragement to those of us experiencing a sense of dislocation in the world—and perhaps seeking an unhealthy sense of longing for another life—that paradise has a place in this world. Ibn Taymiyyah goes further than this, of course, and says that it is only those of us who experience the paradise of this world who can experience the Paradise of the Hereafter. But do not be fooled into thinking that such a state is obtained simply by bowing and prostrating on a prayer mat; or indeed that those experiencing one form or another of melancholy are in a low state of *imān*. Human states, whether spiritual, psychological or emotional are too complex to be facetiously and superficially categorised in this way; there are no simple formulas for bringing about different states of mind and being. However, there is a point to take from the comparison of the Paradise of the Hereafter and the paradisical state which Ibn Taymiyyah believes can be achieved in the life of this world. The Paradise of the Hereafter is a timeless place, in which there is no past and no future—therein only the present exists. It is quite possible, therefore, that the experience of peace, prosperity and happiness in the Paradise of the Hereafter is a consequence of living in and embracing the moment. In Paradise, there will be no place for anxiety over what has passed or anxiety of what is yet to pass. And for this very reason, there will be no disruption to the experience of peace, prosperity and happiness. Now, although living in the present—in the here-and-now—is no doubt something that requires a certain degree of conscious effort, and probably impossible to sustain for long, it is surely a desideratum to be sought, however and whenever possible, if even to momentarily enjoy the taste of what is promised to us in the Paradise of the Hereafter. In the words of another sage: 'Yesterday is history, tomorrow is a mystery, and today is a gift ... that is why it is called the present!' And God knows best!

3

Communion and Division

فَإِنَّ الْجَمَاعَةَ رَحْمَةٌ وَالْفُرْقَةَ عَذَابٌ

Communion is mercy, division is torment.[10]

The spirit of brotherhood, unity, co-operation and mutual support serves to reinforce a sense of communion within the House of Islam. Each is a manifestation of mercy, and where these exist, there exists communion; when these are absent, the resultant state of affairs is division, with torment being a most undesirable corollary. The Qur'an encourages believing men and believing women to treat one another as more than friends—it exhorts believers to treat one another as family. For blood ties are not severed so easily; the bond of friendship, however, can and does. When friendships fall apart, old friends can be replaced by new friends. When

---

10. *Ibn Taymiyya: Against Extremisms*, p. 28.

family ties are ruptured, no mother, father, brother or sister can ever be replaced. It is no doubt because of this fact that most family disputes will always eventually be resolved—sooner or later. Those who are experiencing or have experienced a family dispute will know the urgency felt by all actors involved to reach a resolution. There is a sense in which, ultimately, family *has* to get along. It is with this in mind that the believing community is entreated to view one another as members of the same family. After all, this is the House of Islam, not a clique representing the narrow interests of its individual members. Communion is built upon expressions of mercy; but communion in turn spawns mercy. And thus is created a virtuous cycle, in which communion and mercy are in a beautifully formed symbiotic relationship, in which each reinforces the existence of the other. Division, in contrast, is spawned by hate—not any hate, for there is always a degree to which hate is an important, even vital, human response. It is the level of hate which its bearer struggles to get a grip on; hate which has become so overpowering it begins to torment. Such a state of affairs can lead only to separation. But separation, especially of the absolute kind, is a cause in itself of torment. And thus is created a vicious cycle of negative emotion and negative energy, which if not resolved has the power to be both destructive and self-destructive. But it also renders those involved vulnerable to attack from without. And here lies the greatest challenge facing the Muslim community; a challenge that has arguably confronted it since its emergence. In the words of *Shaykh al-Islām* Ibn Taymiyyah, the champions of solidarity are the true orthodox Muslims:

> How could it be acceptable for the community of Muhammad ﷺ to divide and diverge to such a point that one of their members is an ally of one group [from among them] while concurrently being an enemy of another group, all on account of opinion and passion, without any proof from God? God has made His Prophet ﷺ, innocent of whoever is this way inclined. For such is the way of the inventors of religion, on the pattern of the *Khārijīs* who divided the community of Muslims and judged it lawful to shed the blood of whoever took a position against them. As for the adherents of the Sunnah and the Community, they preserve themselves by taking hold, all together, of the rope of God.[11]

And God knows best!

---

11. *Ibn Taymiyya: Against Extremisms*, p. 27.

4

Innovation

إِنَّ الْبِدَعَ مُشْتَقَّةٌ مِنْ الْكُفْرِ

Innovations are derivatives of disbelief.[12]

It is a malady of the heart that steers a person towards innovations in religion. According to *Shaykh
al-Islām* Ibn Taymiyyah, the three social classes—
ruling elite, *ulama* and the general public—are each
drawn towards inventing new forms of religion
because of their own failure to adhere to the precepts
of the Divine law. The innovations of the ruling elite
include oppressive laws which they promulgate,
such as non-Shar'ī fines and taxes; these stem from
their neglect to enjoin good and forbid evil. If they
demanded only what is Divinely sanctioned for
them to collect and, thereafter, distributed this in

---

12. *Iqtidā' al-ṣirāṭ al-mustaqīm, mukhālafat aṣḥāb al-jaḥīm*,
p. 340.

accordance with Divine law, seeking thereby to consolidate God's religion rather than themselves; if they exacted punishment on the rich as well as the poor, thereby instilling in the hearts of all a mindful awareness of God; they would have no need to expropriate the wealth of their citizenry. As for the *ulama*, if they adhered to the Qur'an and the Sunnah, they would have found therein all that they need of useful knowledge. They would not fall into the errors of the theologians or fall prey to the speculations of jurists, each of whom are led from one unreliable judgment to another. And as for the general public, if only they worshipped their Lord by way of the words and actions taught by Him through His revelation to them, they would reach all of the spiritual stations to which they aspire. They would not feel compelled to replace the recitation of the Qur'an with listening to musical instruments, or to replace Prophetic invocations with invented litanies.

Shaykh al-Islām accepts that some of those who engage in innovations experience spiritual states. This is predictable because every innovation is but an extension of a sanctioned religious practice, such as meditation, fasting or prayer. Some innovations may even be the result of erroneous juridical interpretations of Scripture. In this case, those people who engage in innovation because of a faulty *ijtihād* will be rewarded for those aspects of the new act that have a legally valid foundation and forgiven for those elements which might be considered in the strictest sense *bid'ah*. It should be borne in mind, however, that praiseworthy aspects of an act of inno-vation are outweighed by the blameworthy aspects; and any act in which the blameworthy aspects are preponderant over the praiseworthy are *ipso facto* shunned by the Divine law (*Iqtidā'*, p. 341). Now since any assessment of the harms and benefits of an act requires a perceptive mind and a grounding in religious knowledge, the general public are encouraged to cling to the Qur'an and the Sunnah and avoid if possible innovations in religion. *Shaykh al-Islām* Ibn Taymiyyah warns further that innovations derive from disbelief (*mushtaqq min al-kufr*). Every innovation has the capacity to divert people away from the worship of God alone and from following the Sunnah; furthermore, every innovation supplants a sanctioned rite of worship. If innovations are left to proliferate without curtailment, the result will be the eventual corruption and distortion of the religion of Islam. And God knows best!

5

Real Love

وَأَمَّا مَحَبَّةُ الرَّبِّ سُبْحَانَهُ لِعَبْدِهِ فَقَالَ تَعَالَى: ... (يُحِبُّهُمْ
وَيُحِبُّونَهُ)... وَهَذِهِ الْمَحَبَّةُ حَقٌّ كَمَا نَطَقَ بِهَا الْكِتَابُ
وَالسُّنَّةُ وَالَّذِي عَلَيْهِ سَلَفُ الْأُمَّةِ وَأَئِمَّتُهَا وَأَهْلُ السُّنَّةِ
وَالْحَدِيثِ وَجَمِيعُ مَشَايِخِ الدِّينِ الْمُتَّبَعُونَ وَأَئِمَّةُ التَّصَوُّفِ
أَنَّ اللَّهَ سُبْحَانَهُ مَحْبُوبٌ لِذَاتِهِ مَحَبَّةً حَقِيقِيَّةً

Concerning the love of the Lord for His servants, the
Exalted has said: 'He will love them, and they will love
Him.' This love is real. The Book and the Sunnah speak
of it, and the position of the Salaf of the community
and of its imams, of all the shaykhs of religion who are
followed and the imams of Sufism, is that God, Glorified
is He, is lovable, for His essence, with a real love.[13]

---

*F*or many of us, proclaiming 'I love you, God' is a
statement which rolls off the tongue very easily.

---

13. *Ibn Taymiyya: Against Extremisms*, p. 131.

There is a sense in which 'love' and 'God' are naturally associated. In much the same way, 'I love you, mum' or 'I love you, dad' are said with the utmost ease. Again, the words 'mum', 'dad' and 'love' are naturally associated. And when the Qur'an is read for descriptions of God, and the high frequency of descriptions of Him as merciful, loving and compassionate are encountered, the automatic association of love with God becomes further re-inforced. How beautifully simple it is when religion is kept both uncomplicated and intuitive! Unfortunately, when theologians, philosophers and scholastics get down to the business of constructing creedal systems that purport to explain all the profound questions of how, why and what our relationship with God is, all too often in the process the intuitive ways of thinking and talking about God which are common to the masses are labelled heretical. So, for example, we read in Ashʿarī theology that a servant cannot love God, for that would be too blasphemous; they can only love God's commands. On the other hand, we read that it is impossible for God to love His servants because that would entail some need on God's part for His creatures. It should be of little surprise that such interventions lead people to feel a discomfiting sense of alienation from God. If only these *kalām*-theologians and philosophers would take a moment to read the story of Moses and the shepherd, a story used by Mawlānā Rūmī to highlight how harmful the interference of religious elite in the lives of every-day believers can be. In this story, Moses comes by a shepherd on his knees with his hands spread out to the sky, praying. Although delighted at first, Moses soon hears the shepherd's prayer: 'Oh, my beloved God, I love You more than You can know. I will do anything for You, just say the word. Even if You asked me to slaughter the fattest sheep in my flock in Your name, I would do so without hesitation. You would roast it and put its tail fat in Your rice to make it more tasty. Afterward I would wash Your feet and clean Your ears and pick Your lice for You. That is how much I love You.' Besides himself in anger, Moses interrupts the shepherd and accuses him of sheer blasphemy. Ashamed by what he has done, the shepherd apologises repeatedly and promises to pray as decent people do. Later Moses hears God's voice: 'Oh Moses, what have you done? You scolded that poor shepherd and failed to realise how dear he is to Me. He might not be saying the right things in the right way, but he is sincere. His heart is pure and his intentions good. I am pleased with him. His words might be blasphemy to your ears, but to Me they are sweet blasphemy.'[14] But it is all too late, since the shepherd's relationship with God has now been ruined. In his own way, *Shaykh al-Islām* also wants to bring to the fore the importance of protecting the belief of the masses, in this case by defending a doctrine of love against the interventions of a scholarly elite who preach

---

14. Taken from Elif Shafak's, *The Forty Rules of Love* (Penguin Books, 2010), p. 56.

to the rest that the term love, when used in the Qur'an and Sunnah, is but a metaphor for God's will. Against this, Ibn Taymiyyah argues not just for the possibility, and even necessity, of affirming that God loves—he argues that God's love is one aspect of the fundamental bond between the Creator and the creation. And God knows best!

6

Belief as an Instinct

الْإِقْرَارُ بِالْخَالِقِ وَكَمَالِهِ يَكُونُ فِطْرِيًّا ضَرُورِيًّا فِي حَقِّ مَنْ
سَلِمَتْ فِطْرَتُهُ... وَقَدْ يَحْتَاجُ إِلَى الْأَدِلَّةِ عَلَيْهِ كَثِيرٌ مِنَ
النَّاسِ عِنْدَ تَغَيُّرِ الْفِطْرَةِ وَأَحْوَالٍ تَعْرِضُ لَهَا.

To affirm and to recognise the Creator is an instinct
implanted into the soul of every human being. However,
a person's instinct might become distorted, in which
case he will be in need of rational proofs to arrive at
knowledge of the Divine.[15]

For every compelling argument seeking to prove the
existence of God, there is a counter-argument that
will seem just as compelling. Every thesis, it is true,
has its antithesis. Two examples will suffice. The
ontological argument—that it is possible to imagine

---

15. Wael Hallaq, 'Ibn Taymiyya on the Existence of God', *Acta
Orientalia LII*, p. 58.

a perfect being; such a being could not be perfect unless its essence includes existence; therefore a perfect being exists—has its counter-argument in the form, a perfect being cannot simply be imagined into existence. The causal argument—that everything must have a cause, however it is impossible to have an infinite regression of causes for every existing thing, so there must be a first cause, which itself exists without cause—has its counter-argument in the form, to posit an uncaused first cause undermines the premise of the causal argument. Belief in the existence of God, when based only on reason is therefore extremely vulnerable. Yet despite this fact, Muslim theologians have been undeterred, maintaining that belief in God must be predicated on one or more rational proofs if it is to be considered meaningful. Some even go as far as to say that salvation depends on this. This intransigence on the part of theologians has always been dangerous to the belief of the common man, but never more so than it is today.

Shaykh al-Islām Ibn Taymiyyah's intervention in this debate therefore comes as a breath of fresh air. While he accepts that reason has its place in proving God's existence, *Shaykh al-Islām* believes that this path is only for those people whose natural instinct, or *fiṭrah*, has become corrupted. For the sound, uncorrupted souls, God's existence is known through *fiṭrah*, an innate faculty of perception which stands in contrast to the learnt methods of reasoning that bring perceptions to our minds. Through *fiṭrah* we can know right from wrong, truth from falsehood.

The *fiṭrah* has the potential to see the light of truth and by it we come to acknowledge not only God's existence, but also His omnipotence, greatness and superiority to everything else in the universe. *Shaykh al-Islām*'s position is explained beautifully by Wael Hallaq:

> Just as we know with certitude that there is a sun when we observe its light, we also know that there is a personal God once we see *any one* of a multitude of Signs. Everything in the world is a Sign of the Creator, be it an insect, a sun, a stone, a river, a mountain, etc. The Signs are innumerable, and each and every one points to the one and only Creator. God is seen in every Sign, for no Sign can exist without having been created by Him. Accordingly, there exists for Ibn Taymiyyah an ontological and logical relation of necessary concomitance (*talāzum*) between God and any given Sign, and the apprehension of this concomitance tolerates no doubt whatsoever.[16]

And God knows best!

---

16. Wael Hallaq, 'Ibn Taymiyya on the Existence of God', *Acta Orientalia LII*, pp. 58-59.

A Loving Heart

وَالْقَلْبُ إِنَّمَا خُلِقَ لِأَجْلِ حُبِّ اللهِ تَعَالَى وَهَذِهِ الْفِطْرَةُ
الَّتِي فَطَرَ اللهُ عَلَيْهَا عِبَادَهُ

The heart has been created for the sole purpose of
loving God, the Exalted. This is the natural state which
God has implanted within each of His servants.[17]

*T*oo often, the automatic reaction to hearing or
thinking about God is one of fear. Perhaps the reason
for this is that the religious spokespersons in our lives
have used the idea of a fearsome, punitive God to
impose their own will upon us. Constructing God
in such terms has no doubt been instrumentalised
to great effect throughout the history of religions.
Yet how unfortunate this is for those who are led
to believe this of God, for this is certainly not how

---

17. *Ibn Taymiyya: Against Extremisms*, p. 116.

God intended religion to be deployed. Every human is created with a heart capable of loving God; this is the way that God Himself has fashioned the heart. In fact, from the perspective of spirituality, to love God is the sole purpose for the creation of the heart. This is the natural state, or *fiṭrah*, that God has created His servant upon. Unfortunately, this natural state is vulnerable, open to external influences. So the moment that a child begins to understand, they can be subjected to any number of influences which bear upon them in such a way as to alter this natural state. *Shaykh al-Islām* Ibn Taymiyyah reminds us of the tradition of the Prophet ﷺ: 'Every newborn is born according to the primordial nature and his parents make him a Jew, a Nazarene or a Magian' (Bukhārī). This list is not meant to be exhaustive, only indicative. Therefore, the original state might equally be corrupted by parents who think they are raising their child as a Muslim, but in fact are instilling a form of religion that is far removed from Islam.

Shaykh al-Islām says, 'The Messengers, God pray over them and give them peace, were sent to make firm the *fiṭrah* and to perfect it, not to alter it. When the heart loves God alone and dedicates the religion to Him, it is fundamentally not afflicted by love of any other or, a fortiori, by passion ('ishq). If it is afflicted by 'ishq, it is on account of a deficiency in its love of God alone.'[18] *Shaykh al-Islām* further explains, 'None is afflicted by 'ishq except on account

---

18. *Ibn Taymiyya: Against Extremisms*, pp. 118-119.

of deficiency in his realisation of the Divine unity, or *tawḥīd*, and of his faith. Besides that, in the heart that comes back to God and has fear of Him, there are two things that turn it away from ʿ*ishq*. One is its return to God and its love for Him, which is more agreeable and more excellent than every other thing; with the love for God there is indeed no love for a creature that remains in competition with it. The second thing is the heart's fear of God. Fear, which is the contrary of ʿ*ishq*, indeed turns it away.'[19] And so there is always hope that the corrupted heart can recover its original state, even after it has lost the ability to love God; according to *Shaykh al-Islām* fear is one of the medicines for such a heart, but caution must be exercised here since the one who is over-fearful flees what he fears, and this is certainly not what God intends; nor is it healthy for the servant who wants nothing more than to please his Lord. It is therefore essential that in all of a servant's affairs, including their spiritual and emotional states, the middle way is sought. And God knows best!

---

19. *Ibn Taymiyya: Against Extremisms*, p. 119.

Jihad

وَقَدْ ثَبَتَ أَنَّ (الْجِهَادَ) أَفْضَلُ مَا تَطَوَّعَ بِهِ الْعَبْدُ.
وَالْجِهَادُ دَلِيلُ الْمَحَبَّةِ الْكَامِلَةِ

Jihad is the best voluntary deed a servant may undertake. Jihad is the proof of complete love.[20]

Love necessitates that the lover give themselves up
in the cause of their beloved—it requires nothing
less than being ready to undertake jihad. The lover
loves that which the beloved loves and detests
that which the beloved detests; the lover takes as
a friend the friend of the beloved and takes as an
enemy the enemy of the beloved; the lover is pleased
by that which pleases the beloved and angered by
that which angers the beloved; the lover enjoins
whatever the beloved enjoins and forbids whatever

---

20. *Majmūʿ al-fatāwā*, 10: 36.

the beloved forbids. This is all because the lover is in tandem with the beloved. These words are no truer than they are when thought of in the context of the loving servant and God. The servant who, for their acts of love, are the beneficiary of God's own love for them, to the extent that God becomes pleased when the loving servant is pleased, and angered when the loving servant is angered. The love in this relationship is perfectly reciprocal. These words of *Shaykh al-Islām* beautifully explain love between man and God. They are words which are intimately tied to the statement of God, spoken via His Prophet ﷺ: 'My slave keeps drawing nearer to me with voluntary works until I love him. And when I love him, I am his hearing with which he hears, his sight with which he sees, his hand with which he seizes, and his foot with which he walks. If he asks Me for anything, I will surely give to him, and if he seeks refuge in Me, I will surely protect him. And I do not hesitate to do anything as I hesitate to take the soul of the believer, for he hates death, and I hate to hurt him.' This statement, for *Shaykh al-Islām*, describes the potential union between the believer and God. And nothing, according to him, brings about such a state as effectively as the act of jihad in the path of God. This requires explanation: God has stated clearly in Scripture that loving Him is the foundation of the religion—the perfection of religion is attained via love, while any deficiency in love results *ipso facto* in a deficiency in religion. About this, the Prophet ﷺ has said: 'The head of the matter is Islam, its central pillar is the prayer, and its peak is jihad in the path of God.' The Prophet ﷺ hereby informs us that jihad is the noblest of all actions—the pinnacle of all good deeds. This is further reinforced by the words of God: 'Do you, perchance, regard the mere giving of water to pilgrims and the tending of the Inviolable House of Worship as being equal to the works of one who believes in God and the Last Day and strives hard (*jāhada*) in God's cause? These are not equal in the sight of God' (*al-Tawbah* 9: 19-22). And there are many more verses and traditions of the Prophet ﷺ that elaborate on the lofty status of jihad as well as those that extol the rank of the *mujāhid*. And God knows best!

Pretentions

وَكَثِيرٌ مِنَ السَّالِكِينَ سَلَكُوا فِي دَعْوَى حُبِّ اللهِ أَنْوَاعًا
مِنْ أُمُورِ الْجَهْلِ بِالدِّينِ، إِمَّا مِنْ تَعَدِّي حُدُودِ اللهِ؛
وَإِمَّا مِنْ تَضْيِيعِ حُقُوقِ اللهِ وَإِمَّا مِنْ ادِّعَاءِ الدَّعَاوَى
الْبَاطِلَةِ الَّتِي لَا حَقِيقَةَ لَهَا

Many of those who travel on the spiritual path have
busied themselves, in their pretension to the love of God,
in diverse kinds of matters ignoring the religion, whether
exceeding the limits of God, or neglecting the rights of
God, or having vain pretensions stripped of reality.[21]

The spiritual path is travelled for many reasons.
There are those who travel it for the purpose it was
established: to ascend spiritually. Then there are
those who travel it for questionable reasons, such

---

21. *Ibn Taymiyya: Against Extremisms*, p. 184.

as seeking fame, reputation, authority or wealth. The latter group is no doubt on a slippery slope. Their true colours are manifested in their arrogance, conceit, partisanship, false humility and other ugly traits and behaviours. They are pretenders who in public wear prayer beads and caps while in private they conceal hatred and envy for the true people of God. To all but themselves their hypocrisy is obvious, even cringeworthy. According to *Shaykh al-Islām* Ibn Taymiyyah, three signs mark them apart. The first is that they busy themselves in diverse kinds of matters, ignoring the religion. So, for example, you will find them suggesting solutions to the problems of the *ummah* not from creative engagement with the Prophetic model, but by blind imitation of traditions, religious and otherwise, which have nothing to do with Islam. In doing so their agenda for revivification in fact disregards Islam. The second is that they exceed the limits of God. How else, when they are often the least connected with the Qur'an, the Sunnah and the sciences of the religion. They point out the supposed transgressions of others while they themselves are engaged in transgressions that are both real and serious. The third is that they neglect the rights of God, which are in fact the rights owed to the servants of God, and so all around them, communities, both Muslim and non-Muslim, suffer while they are busy purifying the self. Yet their preoccupation with the ego is, above all else, a vain pretension stripped of reality, for the best way to overcome the ego is to pay it no attention. The most effective way to subdue the ego is to spend time in the service of others. It is here that the life of *Shaykh al-Islām* is paradigmatic, for even while in prison, in a place where he could be forgiven for being consumed by his own ill fortune, he continued to write for the sake of his brethren, responding to their questions, critiquing misguided scholars, challenging tyrannical rulers, reminding them that in everything there is the hand of God at work. Such is the way of the true Sufi. And God knows best!

10

Perfect Faith

مَا يَفْعَلُ أَعْدَائِي بِي؟ إِنَّ جَنَّتِي وَبُسْتَانِي فِي صَدْرِي.
إِنَّ قَتْلِي شَهَادَةٌ، وَسَجْنِي خَلْوَةٌ، وَنَفْيِي سِيَاحَةٌ

What can my enemies do to me? Paradise is in
my heart—wherever I go, it remains with me. My
imprisonment is spiritual retreat, my execution is
martyrdom, my being exiled from my land
is emigration.[22]

When a person has arrived at an understanding of the
purpose behind their existence—the purpose for
which they were created, their raison d'être in the
world—an incredibly important milestone in life can
be considered to have been reached. So fundamental
is knowledge of this kind that it has been reported
from the mouths of the Prophets and the wise that

---

22. *Al-Wābil al-ṣayyib*, p. 109.

'whoever knows himself, knows his Lord'. Indeed knowledge of the self is one of the highest stations of the spiritual path—perhaps even the most important of its stations, for it is the source of unparalleled peace. To fully appreciate this, one need only consider how discomforting, even traumatic, the absence of meaning and purpose can be, or even how much people are prepared to sacrifice in pursuit of these. Certainly by the time in his life that he was said to have spoken these words, *Shaykh al-Islām* Ibn Taymiyyah had already acquired a deep sense of purpose and realisation of the specific path he was destined for. Because of it, he enjoyed such levels of peace that the greatest scholars and mystics of his time were filled with envy. And while they would have wished to have had the final say on the matter of Ibn Taymiyyah's fate, ultimately Ibn Taymiyyah was the victor. He saw only the hand of God in everything that he experienced. All of the paths to gnosis, whether retreats (*khalwah*) or emigration (*hijrah*) or martyrdom (*shahādah*) which are sought out by spiritual aspirants, and are achieved only after great personal sacrifice, were attained by *Shaykh al-Islām* by simply and sincerely speaking truth and living by it. Ultimately, perhaps his most enduring victory is that he is remembered by history while so many of his opponents are nothing more than dates of birth and death.

Shaykh al-Islām Ibn Taymiyyah remained a bastion of support for his students and disciples even when in prison. They took much from his own continued faith in God, strength of character and submission to whatever fate had in store for him. Ibn Qayyim al-Jawziyyah recounts that *Shaykh al-Islām* would say, 'Even if I paid my gaolers an amount of gold to fill this citadel I am kept in, it would not be equal to the level of thanks I owe for this grace.' He would also say while in prison, 'O God, support me to remember You, to thank You and to worship You in the most perfect way.' Once, he said to Ibn al-Qayyim, at a time both had been imprisoned together, 'The truly imprisoned one is he whose heart has been imprisoned; the truly shackled one is he who has been shackled by his desires.' Ibn al-Qayyim said, 'God knows that I have never seen anyone more cheerful about life than he, despite his general lack of means and his frequent imprisonments. You could see comfort and felicity in his face. Whenever we felt fear or anxiety, or the hardship of life, we would come to him and as soon as we saw him and heard his words all hardship would dissipate.'[23] How wonderful to be able to see in all states—in hardship and in ease—the good. And God knows best!

---

23. *Al-Wābil al-ṣayyib*, p. 109.

II

Consultation

ما نَدِمَ مَنِ اسْتَخَارَ الخَالِقَ، وشاوَرَ المَخْلُوقِينَ

The one who seeks right guidance from the Creator
and consults the creation will never suffer regret.[24]

R egret is undoubtedly one of the most discomfiting
of human feelings. Regrets about education, career,
marriage, parenting, friendship and business are
perhaps the most common, but we can experience the
feeling of regret about virtually anything. Furthermore, we can experience regret over both oppor-
tunities we have missed as well as regret over doing
things that in retrospect we probably should have
avoided. According to some experts, the feeling of
regret for a missed opportunity is far worse than
feeling regret for doing something that was best
avoided, because in the latter case, we can at least
learn from the experience.

---

24. *Al-Wābil al-ṣayyib*, p. 157.

As discomfiting as regret can feel, it is also true that it is an important human emotion, inasmuch as it allows us to take stock of our situation and facilitates making correct decisions in the future. Despite its benefits, however, few of us would be foolish enough to pursue regret as a desideratum; we would probably much rather move through life making the right decisions *ab initio*. It is for this reason that *istikhārah* has always held such a foundational place in Muslim life. Literally meaning 'to seek the good', it is the act of turning to God in prayer to consult Him on a matter for which there are two possibilities or more. The tradition of the Prophet ﷺ in this regard is well-known and is reported in Imam al-Bukhārī's collection. On the authority of Jābir, may God be pleased with him, the Prophet ﷺ taught the Companions to do *istikhārah* in all of their affairs. He would say: 'If one of you has decided on a matter then let him first perform two cycles of prayer, after which he should say:

اللَّهُمَّ إِنِّي أَسْتَخِيرُكَ بِعِلْمِكَ وَأَسْتَقْدِرُكَ بِقُدْرَتِكَ وَأَسْأَلُكَ مِنْ فَضْلِكَ الْعَظِيمِ فَإِنَّكَ تَقْدِرُ وَلَا أَقْدِرُ وَتَعْلَمُ وَلَا أَعْلَمُ وَأَنْتَ عَلَّامُ الْغُيُوبِ اللَّهُمَّ إِنْ كُنْتَ تَعْلَمُ أَنَّ هَذَا الْأَمْرَ (هنا تسمي حاجتك) خَيْرٌ لِي فِي دِينِي وَمَعَاشِي وَعَاقِبَةِ أَمْرِي فَاقْدُرْهُ لِي وَيَسِّرْهُ لِي ثُمَّ بَارِكْ لِي فِيهِ اللَّهُمَّ وَإِنْ كُنْتَ تَعْلَمُ أَنَّ هَذَا الْأَمْرَ (هنا تسمي حاجتك) شَرٌّ لِي

فِي دِينِي وَمَعَاشِي وَعَاقِبَةِ أَمْرِي فَاصْرِفْهُ عَنِّي وَاصْرِفْنِي
عَنْهُ وَاقْدِرْ لِي الْخَيْرَ حَيْثُ كَانَ ثُمَّ أَرْضِنِي بِهِ

O God! I consult You as You are All-Knowing and I
appeal to You to give me power as You are the All-
Powerful; I ask You for Your great favour, for You have
power and I do not, and You know all of the affairs of
the unseen. O God! If You know that this matter (here
the need should be stated) is good for me in my religion,
my livelihood, and for my life in the Hereafter, then
make it my destiny and easy for me to attain. And if You
know that this matter (here the need should be stated) is
harmful for me in my religion, my livelihood and my life
in the Hereafter, then keep it away from me and take me
away from it and choose what is good for me wherever
it is, and thereafter make me pleased with it.

And while an explicit response is not always forth-
coming, many who have employed the *istikhārah*
prayer have reported responses in the form of dreams,
visions or esoteric signs. Without wishing to dismiss
the value of dreams, visions or esoteric signs, it is true
that *istikhārah* alone is not the only way of arriving
at a decision. The other component of *istikhārah*, as
Shaykh al-Islām states, is consultation of the creation.
In this context, creation are those whose experience
one values, such as qualified experts, parents, teachers,
mentors, spouses, children and so on. Consulting
such people in life's affairs is an important element of
the decision making process since it allows one to see
a situation from more than one perspective. Indeed

the likelihood of making the right decision for oneself can be increased exponentially after consultation. But then what is the point of *istikhārah*? *Istikhārah* has the important function of creating the right conditions after a course has been taken: if the course of action leads to desirable results, one turns to God in thanks; if it leads to undesirable results, one knows that God must have intended for a lesson to be learnt, thereby safeguarding oneself from the pain of regret. And God knows best!

The Origin of the Term 'Sufi'

سُئِلَ شَيْخُ الْإِسْلَامِ قَدَّسَ اللهُ رُوحَهُ عَنِ الصُّوفِيَّةِ

Shaykh al-Islām, may God sanctify his soul, was
asked about the origin of the term 'Sufi'.[25]

He replied: The term 'Sufi' was all but unknown among
the first three generations of Muslims. It only gained
currency in the successive period, as shaykhs such as
Imām Aḥmad b. Ḥanbal, Abū Sulaymān al-Dārānī
and others began to speak about it. There has long
been a dispute about the origin of the term, which
is a name denoting a relationship to something, just
like *Qurashī*, *Madanī* and their like. Those who have
said the term relates to the *Ahl al-Ṣuffah* (The People
of the Bench) are incorrect because the term for this

---

25. *Majmūʿ al-fatāwā*, 11: 5-6.

would have to be 'ṣuffī'. Those who have said it relates to the 'foremost row' (al-ṣaff al-muqaddam) before God are incorrect because the term for this would have to be 'ṣaffī'. Those who have said it relates to the 'purest' (ṣafwah) of God's creation are incorrect because the term for this would have to be 'ṣafawī'. Those who have said it relates to Ṣūfah b. Bishr b. Udd b. Ṭābikhah, the Arab tribe which lived on the outskirts of Makkah in ancient times and which was known for its hermits, may well be on firm ground in terms of morphology, however, there is unlikely to be a single Sufi who would be pleased with being linked to a pre-Islamic jāhilī tribe which, in any case, was hardly well-known. The best explanation is that the term relates to the donning of wool (ṣūf), a practice known of the disciples of the Basran, ʿAbd al-Wāḥid b. Zayd, and the disciples of al-Ḥasan al-Baṣrī.

In fact, Basrah was known for an excessive form of asceticism and pietism not witnessed in any of the other great cities. We know of a number of stories told about Basrah's ascetics, some of whom are said to have fainted, or even died, after being overwhelmed by the recitation of the Qur'an. Of course, such states were not known of the Companions and so when news of this phenomenon reached a group of Companions, including Asmā' bint Abū Bakr, ʿAbdullāh b. al-Zubayr and Muḥammad b. Sīrīn, they disavowed the practice. Ibn Sīrīn was of the view that excessive pietism was a mere facade—if the same folk were to be observed listening to a recitation of the Qur'an on a rooftop, the outcome would be altogether different.

Others objected on the basis that excessive pietism is an innovation (*bidʿah*), opposed as it is to what we know of the practice of the Companions. The majority of scholars find excuses for such people—this was the position of Imam Aḥmad b. Ḥanbal and Imam al-Shāfiʿī. However, the states of the Companions were actually mentioned in the Qurʾan (which indicates they are the standard for believers). God says about them: 'For, believers are those who, when God is mentioned, feel a tremor in their hearts, and when they hear His Signs rehearsed, find their faith strengthened, and put (all) their trust in their Lord' (*al-Anfāl* 8: 2); 'God has revealed (from time to time) the most beautiful Message in the form of a Book, consistent with itself, (yet) repeating (its teaching in various aspects): the skins of those who fear their Lord tremble thereat; then their skins and their hearts do soften to the celebration of God's praises' (*al-Zumar* 39: 23); 'Whenever the Signs of (God) Most Gracious were rehearsed to them, they would fall down in prostrate adoration and in tears' (*Maryam* 19: 58); 'And when they listen to the revelation received by the Messenger, thou wilt see their eyes overflowing with tears, for they recognise the Truth' (*al-Māʾidah* 5: 83); and 'They fall down on their faces in tears, and it increases their (earnest) humility' (*al-Isrāʾ* 17:109). And God knows best!

13

Deviant Sufis

النَّاسُ يَعْبُدُونَ اللهَ وَالصُّوفِيَّةُ يَعْبُدُونَ أَنْفُسَهُمْ

The masses worship God while the Sufis
worship themselves.[26]

One of life's great ironies is the self-righteous Sufi,
particularly the type who becomes so preoccupied
with self-purification that, rather than overcoming
the ego, ends up worshipping it. When Sufism is
serving its function it provides a means for the believer
to liberate himself from the self-serving ego such that
he is able to engage in the service of God and His
creation. In fact, the service of God and His creation
is the best means of controlling the ego. Of course
the first stage of the path is to learn about the nature
of the ego, the factors that drive it, and the means to
controlling it, as well as to learn about the actions

---

26. *Madārij al-sālikīn*, 1: 148

beloved to God, and the correct way to undertake them. But when a person on a spiritual path becomes so preoccupied with their ego that they see nothing else apart from themselves, this is simply Sufism out of kilter. On so many levels behaviour of this kind is detestable; and what makes it especially so is that in some cases, people have appropriated for themselves a title that none but God has the right to bestow. To such folk, God has the following warning: 'Do not, then, consider yourselves pure, [for] He knows best as to who is conscious of Him' (*al-Najm* 53: 32). Such behaviour is the embodiment of egoism and should be declared as such. It is to this that *Shaykh al-Islām* is pointing and he should not be misunderstood as declaring Sufism a form of heresy. In fact, he, more than any, valued the role of Sufism in purifying and elevating the soul, and wrote and taught extensively on the subject. But he was also a critical friend, who would never shy away from pointing out the dangers associated with Sufism, particularly of the organised kind. It is here, accepting of course that there are always exceptions to every rule, that one will often find the worst sort of partisanship, arrogance, egoism and abandoning of God and His creatures. In contradistinction, it is often among the masses, among whom Islam remains uncomplicated and intuitive, where one finds true Sufism—the Sufism of love, warmth, selflessness, service, sincerity, honesty, fairness and compassion. And God knows best!

14

On True Annihilation

الْفَنَاءُ ... أَنْ يَفْنَى بِعِبَادَةِ اللهِ عَنْ عِبَادَةِ مَا سِوَاهُ وَبِطَاعَتِهِ
عَنْ طَاعَةِ مَا سِوَاهُ وَبِالتَّوَكُّلِ عَلَيْهِ عَنِ التَّوَكُّلِ عَلَى مَا سِوَاهُ
وِبِرَجَائِهِ وَخَوْفِهِ عَنْ رَجَاءِ مَا سِوَاهُ وَخَوْفِهِ فَيَكُونُ مَعَ
الْحَقِّ بِلَا خَلْقٍ

Fanā' is when one passes away in worship of God
from the worship of all else other than Him. He passes
away in obedience to Him from obedience to whatever is
other than Him, in trust from trusting in anything other
than Him, in hope in Him and fear of God, from hoping
and fearing whatever is not Him. Thus he is with the
Truth rather than with creation.[27]

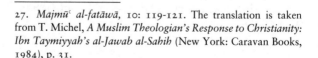

---

27. *Majmūʿ al-fatāwā*, 10: 119-121. The translation is taken
from T. Michel, *A Muslim Theologian's Response to Christianity:
Ibn Taymiyyah's al-Jawab al-Sahih* (New York: Caravan Books,
1984), p. 31.

*F*anā' is one of the most problematic concepts in Sufism. Literally meaning passing-away and effacement, it refers to an important stage of the development of the spiritual aspirant on the path of gnosis. According to *Shaykh al-Islām*, there are two principal ways of understanding *fanā'*. The first is the way of the proponents of *waḥdat al-wujūd*, for whom *fanā'* is the annihilation of the experience of multiplicity, whereby the existence of the creature is the very existence of the Creator. For them, this is the pre-eminent goal of spiritual wayfaring. According to *Shaykh al-Islām*, any such experience has no existence in external reality—it is merely a psychological state which the mystic experiences while in a state of intoxication (*sukr*). The second is the way of the spiritual masters of *Ahl al-Sunnah,* such as Shaykh ʿAbd al-Qādir al-Jilānī. They understand *fanā'* to be the stripping of desire to do other than what God commands, directing the whole range of religious drives only to God. Included within this is to take guidance from God alone (i.e. from the Book and the Sunnah). As *Shaykh al-Islām* says in the statement above, this is true *fanā'*.

Perhaps the best way to understand *fanā'* is through an anecdote from the life of Imam Aḥmad b. Ḥanbal, whom *Shaykh al-Islām* held in high esteem. Imam Aḥmad was once dragged in front of the governor of Baghdad after the Friday prayer to face punishment for the crime of heresy. The imam had refused to sanction the Muʿtazilite doctrine of the created Qur'an imposed by Caliph al-Ma'mūn; he stood instead to uphold the belief of *Ahl al-Sunnah wa al-Jamāʿa*—that the speech of God, the Exalted, is uncreated and eternal. His punishment, on this occasion, was to be whipped a hundred stripes. The person charged with carrying out the punishment began to whip Imam Aḥmad. With every crack of the whip, the only sound audible from the blessed mouth of Imam Aḥmad was the calm repetition of *lā ilāha illā Allāh*. Upon the sixtieth strike, the Imam, who by now had been cut across his body, fell unconscious. Imam Aḥmad was carried back to his home by his distraught students. Upon arrival, he soon regained consciousness. The first thing he wanted to know, to the astonishment of his students, was how long remained until the time for the next prayer. He then asked his students, if they had prayed ʿAṣr. The students replied that they had. 'Help me to make ablution, then prop me up and face me towards Makkah so that I might pray to my Lord', said the Imam to those nearest to him. When he had completed the prayer, his students said to him: 'We are astounded! How is it that, while we were looking on in tears at you being whipped, you were all the while smiling?' The Imam responded: 'As for you all, you could only see the hand of the person charged with lashing me; I, however, could see only the hand of my Lord!' Imam Aḥmad had entered into a state of *fanā'*, in which he could see nothing other than God as the singular cause of everything. Rather than the experience being part of a specific spiritual exercise, in the case of Imam Aḥmad it was merely the fruit of his conviction in the Truth and his unshakeable resolve to stand up for it. And God knows best!

Religious Authority

بِالصَّبْرِ وَالْيَقِينِ تُنَالُ الإِمَامَةُ فِي الدِّينِ

With patience and certainty authority in
religion is earnt.[28]

Not everyone aspires to a position of authority,
especially within a sphere as weighty as religion.
However, for those who do wish to be more than
simply faithful adherents, the challenge is to acquire
the necessary qualities that will both lead to and
facilitate the dual roles of teaching and leadership
that constitute authority in Islam. At the fore of
these qualities are patience and certainty, just as
God has informed us in His Divine writ: 'And when
they became steadfast and believed firmly in Our
revelations, We appointed from among them leaders
who guided by Our command' (al-Sajdah 32: 24). It

---

28. *Madārij al-sālikīn*, 1: 153.

has been said in explanation of this verse that when the Children of Israel were steadfast in obeying the commands of God and avoiding His prohibitions, and in affirming the Messengers and following their example, there grew out of them leaders guiding to the truth, calling to goodness, enjoining good and forbidding evil. But what are patience and certainty, and how do they remain relevant in a world which appears to have no place for either? Patience is an active rather than a passive state: it is to make the choice to remain steadfast until a worthy endeavour has been completed or intuition tells us that the time is right to act. Patience pushes against the fundamental human urge of seeking out immediate gratification, which can lead us to abandon a worthy endeavour or make a move towards a thing before the time is right. To exercise patience is no easy thing in a world where every external pressure, social and technological, is pushing us toward immediacy, rapidity and spontaneity; a world where deceleration, patience and immersive attention are seldom allowed an opportunity. Yet if we could create the conditions which allow us the experience of the latter, we might be astonished by the potential that can be unlocked. Certainty, on the other hand, is the rootedness of knowledge in the heart, such that doubt, uncertainty, speculation, error and desire struggle to find their foothold. This is only possible of knowledge which has entered the heart through immersive attention, critical openness and sound instruction; when knowledge is attained through these channels, it is then truly a form that has the potential to empower. And so it is through one's endeavours undertaken with patience, and through certainty of knowledge, that authority is bestowed. And God knows best!

The Friends of God

୨୧

وَلَيْسَ لِأَوْلِيَاءِ اللهِ شَيْءٌ يَتَمَيَّزُونَ بِهِ عَنِ النَّاسِ فِي الظَّاهِرِ
مِنَ الْأُمُورِ الْمُبَاحَاتِ فَلَا يَتَمَيَّزُونَ بِلِبَاسٍ دُونَ لِبَاسٍ إِذَا
كَانَ كِلَاهُمَا مُبَاحًا وَلَا بِحَلْقِ شَعْرٍ ... بَلْ يُوجَدُونَ فِي
جَمِيعِ أَصْنَافِ أُمَّةِ مُحَمَّدٍ صَلَّى اللهُ عَلَيْهِ وَسَلَّمَ إِذَا لَمْ يَكُونُوا
مِنْ أَهْلِ الْبِدَعِ الظَّاهِرَةِ وَالْفُجُورِ فَيُوجَدُونَ فِي أَهْلِ الْقُرْآنِ
وَأَهْلِ الْعِلْمِ وَيُوجَدُونَ فِي أَهْلِ الْجِهَادِ وَالسَّيْفِ
وَيُوجَدُونَ فِي التُّجَّارِ وَالصُّنَّاعِ وَالزُّرَّاعِ.

There is nothing about the Friends of God—the
awliyā'—that outwardly distinguishes them from the
rest of mankind with respect to the permissible. They do
not wear anything specific and neither are they known
to do anything specific with their hair ... instead they
are to be found amongst every category of the
community of Muhammad (except the people of
innovation and sin). They are found amongst the

reciters of the Qur'an, the scholars, soldiers, traders, manufacturers and farmers.[29]

*T*here have always been pretenders claiming to have reached the status of *wilāyah*, or sainthood. Motivations may differ in the case of each, but worldly gain is often at the root of their dishonesty. And today, in an age when religion has fallen prey to capitalistic forces, bought and sold as though it is no more than a commodity, it is little wonder that the numbers of those seeking to profit by religion is swelling; and claimants to sainthood, by extension, are more prevalent than ever before. We hear about their ability to perform miracles, their power to affect the spiritual state of others, their ability to tell the future, their ability to mind read; yet we also wonder why it is that only their closest disciples ever witness these feats. In fact, these 'Friends of God' rely as much on the naivety of Muslims as they do on their own honed imaginations to conjure up such fantastic claims. With this said, it is important for the believer to consider the Qur'an's definition of sainthood, a definition far more inclusive than such people would ever allow: 'Unquestionably, for the Friends of God there will be no fear on them, nor shall they grieve. They are those who believe and who remain conscious of God' (*Yūnus* 10: 62-63). *Shaykh al-*

---

29. *Majmūʿ al-fatāwā*, 11: 92.

Islām explains that the servant can never attain to faith and God-consciousness unless he seeks to draw close to God; and he can only draw close to God by performing the obligations required of him by Divine law and by avoiding the prohibitions set out therein. Thereafter, the servant continues to draw closer to God by performing supererogatory deeds until he becomes one of the forerunners (*sābiqūn*). Based on this, anyone who claims sainthood for himself while failing to perform the obligations of the religion and failing to avoid its prohibitions, with no will to perform supererogatory acts of goodness or will to avoid what is reprehensible, should never be taken seriously. In fact, it is a sin, according to *Shaykh al-Islām*, for anyone to believe that such a person is a saint. Thus the definition of sainthood in the thought of *Shaykh al-Islām*, which is essentially rooted in the Qur'anic verse, is incredibly important for us to reflect on. It is both powerful and democratic, making it especially relevant in the context of the present day. It is also a definition which is very much consistent with the general tenor of Ibn Taymiyyah's approach to Islam. For him, Islam is a religion which is not the preserve of an elite but rather one that should remain accessible to all—the rich and the poor, the black and the white, the young and the old, the Arab and the non-Arab, man and woman. And God knows best!

17

The Just State

إِنَّ اللهَ يُقِيمُ الدَّوْلَةَ الْعَادِلَةَ وَإِنْ كَانَتْ كَافِرَةً،
وَلَا يُقِيمُ الظَّالِمَةَ وَإِنْ كَانَتْ مُسْلِمَةً

God will support the just state even if it is led by
disbelievers, and He will abandon the oppressive state
even if it is led by believers.[30]

*I*n Islam, justice is understood to mean putting
things in their rightful place. Its opposite, injustice,
applies to any situation in which something has
been misplaced. It is impossible to overstate the
centrality of justice in Islam, and we should expect
nothing less when we pause to consider just how
destructive a force in society injustice is. At every
level of society, from the organisation and running
of the state to the organisation and running of the
home, justice should be the organising principle;

---

30. *Majmūʿ al-fatāwā*, 28: 63.

yet, unfortunately, too often, legalism and stubborn adherence to predetermined rules and norms can make justice seem a distant reality. At the level of state governance, many self-declared Muslim countries score unacceptably low against shared standards of justice, despite having Islamic law enshrined within their constitutions and legal codes. In contradistinction, many so-called non-Muslim countries, which are to all intents and purposes secular, have established such levels of justice that one might be forgiven for wondering whether they are more Islamic than Muslim nations. This state of affairs is understandably confounding many Muslims today, large numbers of whom find it difficult to reconcile the paradox. It is here that *Shaykh al-Islām*'s intervention is particularly relevant, because his statement above, and others of its kind—for example, 'Justice is the organising principle of all things; if the affairs of this world are organised with justice, then even when a non-Muslim is in charge, order will prevail. If the affairs of this world, however, are not organised with justice, then even if a Muslim is in charge, no order can ever prevail'—remind us that our ultimate aim vis-a-vis the political should not be to establish a particular form of state, but rather to establish a particular order—one in which fairness and fair outcomes are secured for all. The state is but an instrument for achieving such an order, it is not an end in itself. With this in mind, it matters not whether justice is brought about by Muslims or non-Muslims, by people of faith or no faith—what matters is that justice exists, and in such a situation, the support of God is to be expected. Equally, when injustice is the status quo, it is of no consequence whether a state is Islamic, with a Muslim leader in charge of its affairs, since God does not lend support to a state that is unjust. And God knows best!

18

Takfīr

وَلَا يَجُوزُ تَكْفِيرُ الْمُسْلِمِ بِذَنْبٍ فَعَلَهُ وَلَا بِخَطَأٍ أَخْطَأَ فِيهِ
كَالْمَسَائِلِ الَّتِي تَنَازَعَ فِيهَا أَهْلُ الْقِبْلَةِ

It is not permissible to call a Muslim an 'unbeliever',
neither for a sin which he has committed nor for anything about which he was in error, such as questions
about which the People of the Qiblah dispute.[31]

S haykh al-Islām Ibn Taymiyyah, in contradistinction
to claims made by his detractors, was vehemently
against excommunication, *takfīr*, of co-religionists.
In this statement, he expressly mentions the im-
permissibility of excommunicating someone for
a sin—here he refutes the judgementalism of the
Khawārij. Notwithstanding that, *Shaykh al-Islām*,
like generations of theologians before him, was
cognisant of the inextricable relationship between

---

31. *Ibn Taymiyya: Against Extremisms*, p. 234.

excommunication and orthodoxy. But what is abundantly clear from his many fatwas and epistles is that he had a systematic approach to *takfīr*, whether it be for a major issue such as disbelief (*kufr*) or a minor issue such as a sin (*fisq*). He would also regularly substantiate the canons of excommunication with legal maxims, such as the rule, 'No one has the right to excommunicate any Muslim until proof can be verified against him; if a person's Islam has been established with certainty, then it should not be disclaimed for mere doubt' (*Majamū' al-fatāwā*, 2: 466).

Shaykh al-Islām arguably articulated those issues which guard against excommunication more succinctly than many other theologians. Among the things which present a barrier to excommunication, according to him, are: recent conversion; having access only to heterodox scholars and hence following them; having bouts of madness or intellectual deficiency; lacking access to the statutes backed by the Book and the Sunnah; and coercion. In this respect, *Shaykh al-Islām* sets out grades of heterodoxy: 'The many factions associating themselves with speculative theology (*uṣūl al-dīn wa al-kalām*) are of varying categories. Some of them may have contravened orthodoxy in major issues, whilst others on subtle issues' (*Majamū' al-fatāwā*, 3: 348). *Shaykh al-Islām* argues that Imam Aḥmad supplicated and sought forgiveness for the caliphs al-Ma'mūn and al-Muʿtaṣim, both of whom subscribed to the doctrine of the 'created Qur'an', which in generic terms was declared a statement of unbelief by the Pious Predecessors. According to *Shaykh al-Islām*, if they were disbelievers or apostates then it would not have been permissible for Imam Aḥmad to seek forgiveness on their behalf (*Majamūʿ al-fatāwā*, 12: 389-488).

To regulate open-ended takfīrism, *Shaykh al-Islām* limited the social exclusion of heterodox believers to polemical refutations, transmission of knowledge, and boycotting (*hajr*). Regarding polemical refutations, even though *Shaykh al-Islām* refuted the Ashʿarīs, he argued that 'they are the closest of the heterodox sects to orthodoxy.' As for taking knowledge from non-Sunnis, *Shaykh al-Islām* maintained that every faction possesses truth and falsehood—it is obligatory to follow the truth that they speak and reject the falsehood thereof. Boycotting a believer, according to the Shaykh, can be done as a punitive measure as the Prophet Muhammad ﷺ did with the three Companions who remained behind in the Battle of Tabūk: 'God turned in mercy also to the three who were left behind; they felt guilty to such a degree that the earth seemed constrained to them, for all its spaciousness, and their very souls seemed straitened to them. And they perceived that there is no fleeing from God, and no refuge, but to Himself. Then He turned to them, that they might repent: for God is Oft-Returning, Most Merciful' (*al-Tawbah* 9: 118). This too though should be considered within the ambit of public interest. Moreover, *Shaykh al-Islām* concludes that there are issues which do not warrant minor heresy let alone major excommunication. As evidence he cites the dispute among the Companions as to whether the Prophet ﷺ saw God. And God knows best!

19

Miracles

وَكَرَامَاتُ أَوْلِيَاءِ اللهِ إِنَّمَا حَصَلَتْ بِبَرَكَةِ اتِّبَاعِ
رَسُولِهِ صَلَّى اللهُ عَلَيْهِ وَسَلَّرَ

The miracles of the *awliyā'*—the Friends of God—are
only attained through following the Messenger,
peace and blessings be upon him.[32]

---

*S*haykh al-Islām Ibn Taymiyyah never disputes the
centrality of the spiritual path in Islam, or the fruits
attained by its wayfarers. Indeed in much of his
writing, there are interesting convergences between
his approach to Sufism and the systems of the
shaykhs of well-known *ṭuruq*. This said, his epistles
on spirituality should not be read as handbooks of
Sufism since *Shaykh al-Islām* is ambivalent about
the precise nature of the system he envisages for a

---

32. *Majmūʿ al-fatāwā*, 11: 305.

spiritual aspirant. On the one hand, he implies that every wayfarer should have a shaykh, linked in a line of shaykhs back to the Prophet ﷺ; on the other, he does not state anywhere that a disciple should commit to a particular spiritual order. What, then, was *Shaykh al-Islām* proposing with his construction of the spiritual path? It is clear that *Shaykh al-Islām* wants spirituality, and religious practice generally, to be rooted in the Qur'an and the Sunnah of the Prophet ﷺ; the latter dimension means to be based strictly on the soundly-reported Hadiths, especially those collected in the *Ṣiḥāḥ*. In this way, he sought to position the personality of the Prophet ﷺ at the fore of the spiritual path in order to effectively create a model of authority in which sainthood and religious leadership would be predicated on the imitation of the Prophetic archetype. In the outlook of *Shaykh al-Islām*, attention on the Prophet ﷺ essentially means an emphasis upon the Shariah before anything else. Ultimately, he sought a rapprochement between the Shariah and *ḥaqīqah*, which he taught could be achieved through close study of the religious observances of the Prophet ﷺ as recorded in the sound traditions (*ṣiḥāḥ*). Only from the Prophetic tradition could there follow an authentic model of *Imitatio Muḥammadi*; spiritual practices which could not be justified by the texts of the Qur'an and Hadith were to be condemned as innovations.

Against this backdrop, the true *awliyā'*, or Friends of God, are those who follow the Prophet Muhammad ﷺ, observing fastidiously those things which he commanded and avoiding those things which he prohibited. According to *Shaykh al-Islām*, 'They follow the Prophet ﷺ in that which God has revealed, and hence He aids them with His angels and a spirit from Him. He places His light in their hearts and honours them with miracles. The miracles of the elite from among the *awliyā'* are performed for the benefit of Faith or to fulfill the needs of the Muslims, just as the miracles of their Prophet ﷺ were performed for this end.' How far removed are such people from those charlatans who perform miracles for reputation and wealth, who are able to perform extraordinary feats but who in reality could not be further away from the spiritual path. And how dangerous when people observe at their hands miracles which are then taken as signs of sainthood (*wilāyah*). The mistake of the masses is that they erroneously believe that every extraordinary act constitutes a saintly miracle and is *ipso facto* a sign indicating sainthood. They are unable to discern the Friends of God from the Friends of Satan. In fact, miracles are of types: the prophetic miracle (*mu'jizah*), the saintly miracle (*karāmah*) and the false miracle (*istidrāj*). This last category, according to Sufi masters, is one that people must be heedful of. *Istidrāj* occurs at the hands of charlatans who acquire the ability to make the extraordinary happen. The miracle is false because it serves to both further the self-deception of the one performing it— he becomes convinced of his own *wilāyah*—and it also deceives onlookers into believing that such a person is a saint. The differences between the three categories of miracle are subtle and they can certainly not be told apart by the fundamental nature of the act. Indeed, only close scrutiny of the performer can reveal the true nature and quality of the act he performs. And God knows best!

20

True Intelligence

لَيْسَ الْعَاقِلُ الَّذِي يَعْلَمُ الْخَيْرَ مِنَ الشَّرِّ وَإِنَّمَا الْعَاقِلُ
الَّذِي يَعْلَمُ خَيْرَ الْخَيْرَيْنِ وَشَرَّ الشَّرَّيْنِ

The intelligent man is not the one who knows good
from evil. The intelligent man is the one who knows the
better of two goods and the worse of two evils.[33]

An ability to relay a list of the lawful and the
prohibited in Islam is hardly an impressive skill, and
says virtually nothing about a person's intelligence,
however much someone might want to believe it
does. The most that this requires is to find a list
(which is hardly difficult in the age of the Internet)
and then proceed with committing the list to memory.
Barely any mental energy beyond this is needed.
Notwithstanding this fact, there are still far too

---

33. *Ibn Taymiyya: Against Extremisms*, p. 258.

many so-called "religious police" within the Muslim community who are ready to make interventions in the lives of fellow-believers, pointing out their mistakes—whether a perceived contravention of a prohibition or a perceived failure to perform an obligation—often in a way that is patronising or that smacks of arrogance. Little thought is given by these religious police to the circumstances of the (often) unsuspecting recipient of their directives: no thought as to whether the recipient may actually already be knowledgeable about the same list of dos and don'ts but has some mitigating reason for acting in a way contrary to the list. Does the thought ever cross the mind of these self-appointed police that their target may actually be doing what, in the sight of God, is preferable? Have they not thought that perhaps their target is in a situation where they have had to choose between the better of two goods or the lesser of two evils?

Shaykh al-Islām highlights that the ability to discern the better of two goods or the lesser of two evils is the true measure of a believer's intelligence. This makes sense, of course, when one considers the tools necessary for determining subtle differences between two seemingly analogous possibilities and for which conditions do not allow the overcoming of the problem by either undertaking both goods, or avoiding both evils. For a person in this situation, there are rarely any easy exit strategies, and while it may be possible to consult a religious authority, it is still ultimately for the person confronted with the situation to decide on how they will proceed. While there are a number of important tools that a person might want to deploy for such a task, certainly the most important is intuition, or *firāsah*. The Prophet ﷺ often spoke about *firāsah* to his Companions. On one occasion, he said, 'Be warned of the *firāsah* of the believer, for he sees by the light of God' (Tirmidhī). Intuition is something that we all possess, and will all fall back on in our daily lives. Few of us, however, are confident enough to allow it to guide us through our religious dilemmas. This is a shame because it means that we may not be making the best possible decision for ourselves, especially in cases in which the advice we receive following consultation conflicts with our gut feeling. It is of course perfectly Islamic to allow our intuition to guide us, and at moments when we lack the confidence to fall back on our innate ability to navigate a course through moral dilemmas, let us recall the beautiful statement of the Prophet ﷺ: 'Consult your heart. Goodness is that about which the soul feels at ease and the heart feels tranquil. And evil is that which wavers in the soul and causes uneasiness in the breast, even though people have given you their verdict on it' (Aḥmad). And God knows best!

21

Sins

فَإِنَّ الْمَعَاصِيَ قَيْدٌ وَحَبْسٌ لِصَاحِبِهَا عَنِ الْجَوَلَانِ فِي فَضَاءِ
التَّوْحِيدِ وَعَنْ جَنْيِ ثِمَارِ الْأَعْمَالِ الصَّالِحَةِ

Sins are like chains and locks preventing their
perpetrator from roaming the vast garden of *Tawḥīd*
and reaping the fruits of righteous actions.[34]

The Islamic conception of sin is perhaps unique among
world religions. Sin is constructed not as a frailty *per
se* but rather as an opportunity for transformation—
it is a means to learn about oneself, creating the possibility of becoming a better human being. In Islam,
sinning is part of the human condition. The Prophet
ﷺ said, 'I swear by Him in whose hand is my soul,
if you were a people who did not commit sin, God
would take you away and replace you with a people

---

34. *Diseases of the Hearts and Their Cures*, p. 28.

who would sin and then seek God's forgiveness so He could forgive them' (Muslim). Yet sin can also be an inhibiting force, especially when it gives birth to shame, an emotion which can, if ignored, become quite paralysing, and even destructive in our lives. Brené Brown explains that shame is the intensely painful feeling or experience of believing that we are flawed and therefore unworthy of love and belonging.[35] In this sense, shame is all about fear. The opposite of shame though, is courage: to take ownership of your story, the good and the bad, and to weave for yourself a story of success. This is much closer to the Divine opportunity instilled in sin. Of course we have to accept that shame is an undesirable, even harmful emotion, but equally, there has to be an acknowledgment both that sin exists and our personal responsibility when it happens.

When sin prevents someone from reconnecting with faith, and roaming the vast gardens of *tawḥīd* to reap the fruits of righteous action, the problem is usually from a lack of space for the sinning person to speak about the conditions that led them to sin, to talk honestly about the nature of their sin and the opportunity to the practical ways to overcome it. Two key issues are obstacles to this: first, the belief that sins are not to be spoken about with anyone under any circumstances; second, people are not willing to

---

35. B. Brown, *The Gifts of Imperfection* (Minnesota: Hazelden, 2010), p. 39.

accept personal responsibility in an age when victim-hood seems to be the order of the day.

Finally, what are the gardens of *tawḥīd* that *Shaykh al-Islām* refers to? They are the occasions and locations in which a believer experiences profound connection with God. They are the occasions and locations in which righteous actions are performed, and in which remorse for misdeeds is expressed, for the sake of God alone. It is these that produce the fruits of faith. And God knows best!

22

Sincerity

الشَّفَاعَةُ: سَبَبُهَا تَوْحِيدُ اللهِ وَإِخْلَاصُ الدِّينِ وَالْعِبَادَةِ بِجَمِيعِ أَنْوَاعِهَا لَهُ فَكُلُّ مَنْ كَانَ أَعْظَمَ إِخْلَاصًا كَانَ أَحَقَّ بِالشَّفَاعَةِ كَمَا أَنَّهُ أَحَقُّ بِسَائِرِ أَنْوَاعِ الرَّحْمَةِ

It is in accordance with a servant's commitment to
taw̄ḥīd and being sincere in faith to God that he
deserves the generosity of God in the form of
intercession and other graces.[36]

*I*f a servant hopes to be graced with the bounties
enjoyed by the Friends of God, he needs to work
towards internalising a deep and meaningful sense
of *taw̄ḥīd* (monotheism). The process of internal-
isation can only happen when he attains sincerity
in faith (*ikhlāṣ*), about which the Qur'an in several

---

36. *Majmūʿ al-fatāwā*, 10: 31.

instances speaks directly: 'And call upon Him, making your devotion sincere' (al-Aʿrāf 7: 29); 'And they have been commanded no more than this: To worship God, offering Him sincere devotion, being true [in faith]' (al-Zalzalah 98: 5). Sincerity is, in part, a process of divestiture: one must become detached from the inclinations of the ego and remove all worthless cares; thereafter, one must focus all attention on pleasing God, the Exalted, and undertaking all actions for Him alone. Sincerity might be seen as the nexus between the subjective proclamation of *tawḥīd*, which emanates from the believer, and the objectivised manifestation of *tawḥīd*, which God discloses through visions and illuminations to whomever He wills from among His worshippers. The believer who is constant in his striving to perfect his actions and attain sincerity should not consider experiences of Divine Oneness to be anything but a good sign. There is a caveat, however such experiences must not be a cause for complacency; rather, they should be a motivation and a catalyst for the believer to increase in his striving. And God knows best!

23

Concealing Knowledge

لَا يَجُوزُ التَّوَاطُؤُ عَلَى كِتْمَانِ مَا يُحْتَاجُ إِلَى نَقْلِهِ وَمَعْرِفَتِهِ
لِجَرَيَانِ ذَلِكَ فِي الْقُبْحِ مَجْرَى التَّوَاطُؤِ عَلَى نَقْلِ الْكَذِبِ
وَفِعْلِ مَا لَا يَحِلُّ

The conspiracy to conceal a thing which ought to be
transmitted and made known is impermissible. Such a
thing is as awful as conspiring to transmit a lie and
to do that which is not licit.[37]

S haykh al-Islām Ibn Taymiyyah always taught that
the Righteous Predecessors—the earliest Muslims—
were as the Prophet ﷺ described them: the 'best of
generations.' Among their traits was that they had
trust in the words of God, since they acknowledged,
with absolute certainty, the trustworthy nature of
God Himself. *Shaykh al-Islām* completely rejected

---

37. *Majmūʿ al-fatāwā*, 4: 6.

the views of philosophers like al-Fārābī and Ibn Sīnā who held that the words of God, and even the discourses of His prophets, were sometimes crude and mostly to be read literally as they were aimed at lay people, who would otherwise not grasp their meaning. There should never be any doubt, according to *Shaykh al-Islām*, about the purposefully simplistic language of the Qur'an, and its frequent allusions to the ways of the desert, in a language clear to the Bedouin; notwithstanding this, there should, at the same time, be no doubt about the relationship between the language of revelation and the realities it speaks about. Furthermore, to posit that a prophet of God, by the commissioning of God Himself, would speak lies just to make sense to those of 'lesser intelligence' was simply inconceivable according to *Shaykh al-Islām*, and creates in any case more problems than it solves.

The broader sense in which this statement of *Shaykh al-Islām* can be read is in the context of the learned—especially our scholars—and the duty upon them to inform people of the truth. Citing the famous statement of Imam ʿAlī—'Speak to the people in accordance with their understanding' (Bukhārī)—and claiming that the truth has the potential to lead people astray, many scholars seek to justify their withholding of knowledge from the masses. However, there are a number of ethical considerations here: if knowledge is withheld from people, then this has an impact on their ability to make the right moral choices for themselves;

withholding knowledge makes it the preserve of a few, whereas God intends for it to be available to all; there is a further consequence—the masses remain in a state of immaturity, since they are taught what to think rather than allowed to think for themselves. This also has an impact of course on their moral autonomy, which raises questions about the quality of their belief. And in the age of the internet, one has to question how disconnected those are who continue to believe in the benefit of concealing knowledge. Do they not realise that the information they seek to conceal will either already be available somewhere in cyberspace or will be publicly available at some point in the future. And God knows best!

24

Following Lust

وَمِنَ الْمَعْلُومِ أَنَّ مُجَرَّدَ نُفُورِ النَّافِرِينَ أَوْ مَحَبَّةِ
الْمُوَافِقِينَ: لَا يَدُلُّ عَلَى صِحَّةِ قَوْلِهِ وَلَا فَسَادِهِ إِلَّا إِذَا
كَانَ ذَلِكَ بِهُدًى مِنَ اللهِ

It is known that the mere flight of those that would
flee and the love of those in agreement does not prove
the soundness of a statement or the falsity thereof,
unless it is based on the guidance from God.[38]

Shaykh al-Islām Ibn Taymiyyah's life embodies the
seeking of truth, the defence of truth, and thereafter total reliance on God with respect to the con-
sequences of doing so. In contrast, the lives of so
many of his opponents were driven by agendas not
aiming at truth, but at fame, fortune and power.
Such people, who in the eyes of Shaykh al-Islām

---

38. *Majmūʿ al-fatāwā*, 4: 98.

are but slaves to their lust, must take heed of Divine guidance. Accordingly,

> To take that as a proof would be to do so by following one's lusts without guidance from God, for a person's following of his lusts is his adopting a saying or action which he loves, and rejecting a saying or action which he hates, without having recourse to guidance from God. He—Exalted be He—has said, "But, behold, many lead others astray by their own lusts without knowledge" (*al-Anʿām* 6: 119); and He says, 'But if they respond not to you, then know that they follow only their own lusts: and who is more astray than one who follows his own lusts, devoid of guidance from God' (*al-Qaṣaṣ* 28: 50); and He—Exalted be He—said to Dāwud, "Nor follow lust, for it will mislead you from the path of God" (*Ṣād* 38: 26); and He—Exalted be He—said, 'If they bear witness, then do not bear witness with them: Nor follow the lusts of those who consider Our signs as falsehood or those who believe not in the Hereafter and deem others equal with their Lord' (*al-Anʿām* 6: 150); and He—Exalted be He—said, "Say: O People of the Book! Do not exceed the bounds in your religion beyond what is true, nor follow the lusts of a people who have lost the way in times gone by, who misled many, and had themselves lost the even way" (*al-Māʾidah* 5: 77); and He—Exalted be He—said, 'The Jews and Christians will never be pleased with you until you follow their religion. Say: "The guidance of God is the [only] guidance." Were you to follow

their lusts after the knowledge which has reached you, then you would find no ally or aid against God' (*al-Baqarah* 2: 120). Thus whoever follows the lusts of people after having knowledge of what God has sent His Messenger with, and after knowing of God's guidance which He has made clear to His servants, is of this status. For this reason the ancients would name the people of innovation and schism—those who would contravene the Book and the Tradition—"people of lust", since they accepted what they loved and rejected what they hated by virtue of their lusts, without guidance from God. (*Ibid.*)

And God knows best!

Kalam Theology

تَجِدُ أَهْلَ الْكَلَامِ أَكْثَرَ النَّاسِ انْتِقَالًا مِنْ قَوْلٍ إِلَى
قَوْلٍ وَجَزْمًا بِالْقَوْلِ فِي مَوْضِعٍ وَجَزْمًا بِنَقِيضِهِ وَتَكْفِيرِ
قَائِلِهِ فِي مَوْضِعٍ آخَرَ

You will find that the proponents of *kalām* are the
foremost amongst people in shifting from one position
to another, certain of a position at one place and then
certain of its contrary, all the while accusing
opponents of disbelief![39]

hroughout his career *Shaykh al-Islām* remained ambivalent about the utility of *kalām*, or rational theology. This was in no small part due to the aggressive
and absolutist way that *kalām* was advocated by its
proponents. His fear was both for the religion, and
how it would be impacted by rational theology, but

---

39. *Majmūʿ al-fatāwā*, 4: 14.

also for the masses, and where they would be left if the language of orthodoxy became too elitist. In any case, it was clear to *Shaykh al-Islām* that the best evidence against the people of *kalām* was the fact that they were always shifting from one intellectual position to another, sometimes even ending back at where they began. For him, this all pointed to their lack of certainty. In his words, 'Indeed, faith is as [Heraclius] said, after asking Abū Sufyān about those who had entered Islam with the Prophet ﷺ: "Has any of them returned back from his religion from disillusionment after he has entered it?" To this Abū Sufyān replied no. Caesar then said: 'Such is faith when its countenance graces the hearts; none who has experienced it can be discontented.' For this reason, one of the Pious Predecessors said, "Whoever makes his religion a destination he seeks to arrive at through argumentation is most likely to shift position." As for the adherents of the Sunnah and the traditionists, there are no reports of any of their scholars or their righteous disciples ever having recanted a statement or a doctrine. Rather, they are the greatest of people in steadfastness, even though they may be tried by various trials, and afflicted by various afflictions. This is the state of the Prophets and their followers, such as those who have passed like the People of al-Ukhdūd and their like. So too suffered the ancients of this nation—the Companions and the Followers and others.'[40]

---

40. *Ibid.*

Shaykh al-Islām was very clear about the job of the Muslim theologian: fundamentally, it was to protect the religion against corruption, preserving all the while its pristine simplicity for all. But few theologians do this job, which has resulted in the degeneration of theology as a discipline. In the words of Goldziher, which could quite easily have been penned by *Shaykh al-Islām* himself:

> The theologian answers questions that lie outside the prophet's sphere of interest; he reconciles contradictions the prophet would have been at ease with; he devises inflexible formulas, and erects rows upon rows of argument into ramparts, in the hope of securing those formulas against assault from within and without. He then derives all his systematically ordered tenets from the prophet's words, not infrequently from their most literal sense. He proclaims that those tenets are what the prophet had intended to teach from the outset. Theologian disputes with theologian, each hurling the cunning arguments of an arrogant subtlety at anyone who, using the same means, draws different conclusions from the living words of the prophet.[41]

And God knows best!

---

41. I. Goldziher, *Introduction to Islamic Theology and Law* (New Jersey: Princeton University Press, 1981), p. 67.

26

Figurative Interpretation

وَقَدْ طَالَعْتُ التَّفَاسِيرَ الْمَنْقُولَةَ عَنِ الصَّحَابَةِ وَمَا رَوَوْهُ مِنْ
الْحَدِيثِ وَوَقَفْتُ مِنْ ذَلِكَ عَلَى مَا شَاءَ اللهُ تَعَالَى مِنَ
الْكُتُبِ الْكِبَارِ وَالصِّغَارِ أَكْثَرَ مِنْ مِائَةِ تَفْسِيرٍ فَلَمْ
أَجِدْ - إِلَى سَاعَتِي هَذِهِ - عَنْ أَحَدٍ مِنَ الصَّحَابَةِ أَنَّهُ تَأَوَّلَ
شَيْئًا مِنْ آيَاتِ الصِّفَاتِ أَوْ أَحَادِيثِ الصِّفَاتِ بِخِلَافِ
مُقْتَضَاهَا الْمَفْهُومِ الْمَعْرُوفِ؛ بَلْ عَنْهُمْ مِنْ تَقْرِيرِ ذَلِكَ

I have read all the commentaries which have been
transmitted from the Companions and all the Hadith
reports from them; I have pondered, for as long as
God has willed me to, all the major works and the
minor works, totalling more than a hundred [books],
yet I have not found—until now—that any of the
Companions figuratively interpreted any of the
verses or any of the Hadith which speak about the
attributes in a manner which removes their
meaning from what is customarily understood

by them. Rather, I have only found them to
have affirmed them.[42]

*M*any theologians have claimed that the salaf, while
affirming the attributes of God, at the same time
denied their primary lexical signification. According
to *Shaykh al-Islām*, such a view is erroneous. An
attribute such as 'hand' is connotative, its particular
signification being contingent upon the context in
which it is used and the person to whom it is at-
tributed. So, the primary signification of a word, i.e.
its denotation, is that which first occurs to the native
speaker. It may be based on its original coinage or
the contextual setting in which it is used. To concep-
tualise God's hand as a human limb, or His anger
as an emotionally overpowering urge to avenge a
wrong, or His presence in the heavens to be like that
of water in a cloud, has to be fundamentally flawed
since none of these ideas should come to mind *ab
initio*, especially not to the mind of a believer who
is constantly aware of the reality that nothing is like
unto God—Exalted is He—whether in His essence,
His attributes or His actions. Thus 'hand' to the one
of sound reason is like the attributes of knowledge,
power and existence. In the same way that we do

---

42. *Majmūʿ al-fatāwā*, 7: 196.

not consider our contingent knowledge, contingent
power and contingent existence to be in any way like
the knowledge, power and existence of God, neither
do we deem our hand to be anything like His. The
correct position, according to *Shaykh al-Islām*, is
to say that 'these attributes are attributes of God—
Glorified and Exalted is He—as befits His majesty.
Their ascription to His sanctified being is like the
ascription of the attributes of anything to itself.'
Furthermore, one should only have recourse to the
metaphorical interpretation of a word used by God
to describe Himself when the following conditions
are met: firstly, that the word in question is known
to be used metaphorically in Arabic; this is so since
the Qur'an, the tradition and the discourse of the ancients were in Arabic. If this principle is not upheld,
then it is for anyone to interpret whatsoever he wills,
howsoever he wills; secondly, that there exists an
associated proof which necessitates a metaphorical
understanding rather than a literal one; this proof
should be either logical or one known by tradition;
thirdly, that this same proof must not be in conflict
with another clear indication, whether Qur'anic
or theological, which necessitates that the word in
question should be understood literally; fourthly,
that the Prophet ﷺ has explained it as such: this is
so since it is assumed that the Prophet ﷺ, if speaking
metaphorically, would have made clear to listeners
that he was doing so, especially if his discourse was
of a doctrinal nature requiring the acceptance of
Muslims. This assumption makes sense when one

considers that the Prophet ﷺ was sent as a deputy of God, with His Book, to explain to people the abstruse aspects of revelation. By the sending of Prophets as bearers of the Divine imperative, God, in some sense, absolves Himself of His responsibility towards mankind. So when theologians interpret away various attributes of God which are spoken about in revelation, for our Shaykh there is simply no justification for this. It is only a corrupt mind which would perceive a human-like form for God. The belief of the People of the Sunnah and the Community, is predicated on the certainty that there is nothing like unto God—no co-equal sharing any of His attributes. And God knows best!

27

You Alone We Worship

قَوْلُهُ: (إِيَّاكَ نَعْبُدُ وَإِيَّاكَ نَسْتَعِينُ) . فَهَذَا تَفْصِيلٌ لِقَوْلِهِ:
(الْحَمْدُ للهِ رَبِّ الْعَالَمِينَ) . فَهَذَا يَدُلُّ عَلَى أَنَّهُ لَا مَعْبُودَ
إِلَّا اللهُ وَأَنَّهُ لَا يَسْتَحِقُّ أَنْ يُعْبَدَ أَحَدٌ سِوَاهُ فَقَوْلُهُ:
(إِيَّاكَ نَعْبُدُ) إِشَارَةٌ إِلَى عِبَادَتِهِ بِمَا اقْتَضَتْهُ إِلَهِيَّتُهُ: مِنَ الْمَحَبَّةِ
وَالْخَوْفِ وَالرَّجَاءِ وَالْأَمْرِ وَالنَّهْيِ. (وَإِيَّاكَ نَسْتَعِينُ) إِشَارَةٌ
إِلَى مَا اقْتَضَتْهُ الرُّبُوبِيَّةُ مِنَ التَّوَكُّلِ وَالتَّفْوِيضِ وَالتَّسْلِيمِ

'You alone we worship; You alone we ask for help'
is the elaboration of His saying, 'Praise be to God,
Lord of the worlds.' This indicates that there is
no object of worship except God and that no one
other than Him has the right to be worshipped.
His statement, 'You alone we worship,' points
to worship of Him by means of love, fear, hope,
command and prohibition that His divinity
requires, and, 'You alone we ask for help,'

points to the complete trust, commitment, and
submission that His lordship requires.[43]

*T*he chapter *al-Fātiḥah* is one of the greatest of the
Qur'an's secrets. In seven short, majestic verses
the surah encapsulates the core themes of the one-
hundred and thirteen remaining chapters of the
Qur'an. Unravelling the layers of meaning within
al-Fātiḥah is no easy endeavor and has engaged
the greatest exegetical minds throughout Muslim
history. Each exegete will read the surah from a
different vantage point, depending, among other
things, on their own interests and experience of
life. The best-known interpreters of the Qur'an,
such as Imam Fakhr al-Rāzī, have filled pages of
their commentaries extrapolating and expounding
on its meanings, which never seem to dry up.
Many ordinary believers, who are required to read
this surah at least seventeen times a day as part of
their daily worship, will have developed their own
relationship with *al-Fātiḥah*, understanding it in a
way that is perhaps unique and personal to them.
Ultimately, each one of us will take from *al-Fātiḥah*
whatever God wills for us to take.

Shaykh al-Islām's own interpretation constitutes
a profound contribution to our understanding of

---

43. J. Hoover, *Ibn Taymiyya's Theodicy of Perpetual Optimism*
(Leiden: Brill, 2007), p. 28.

this important surah, and justifies his position among the foremost Muslim minds. Here he explains the significance of the middle verse of *al-Fātiḥah*, 'You alone we worship, You alone we ask for help.' According to *Shaykh al-Islām*, this fifth verse constitutes both the summary of the surah and the pivot between its two halves. The first half of the surah— 'All praise is due to God alone, the Sustainer of all the worlds; the Most Gracious, the Dispenser of Grace; Lord of the Day of Judgment'—emphasises worship dedicated to God. This theme is captured in, 'You alone we worship.' The second half of the surah—'Guide us the straight way; The way of those upon whom You have bestowed Your blessings; Not of those who have been condemned, nor of those who go astray!'—emphasises the relationship between the worshipper and his Lord, in which the worshipper asks for the help that God will provide. Therefore the middle verse encapsulates the two themes of worship and supplication that the whole surah embodies. As Jon Hoover explains,

> For Ibn Taymiyya, asking for help signifies absolute human dependence on the God who is the Lord of the worlds. Lordship indicates God's creative and determining activity, and this Lordship is exclusive. Creatures have absolutely no existence apart from God, and they may ask for help only from the source of their existence and trust in Him alone. The confession that God is the sole Creator and Lord of the universe is called *tawḥīd al-rubūbiyyah* […]. In like

manner, worship indicates human devotion to God—turning to Him, loving Him, obeying Him, hoping in Him and fearing Him—and this is linked to God's divinity (*ulūhiyyah*). The divine is that which is loved and served as a god, and God's divinity denotes His essential right to worship. *Tawḥīd al-ulūhiyyah* [...] is recognizing God as the only one with the right to divinity and turning to worship Him alone. This [...] is the meaning of, "There is no god but God". Unifying all one's energies in worship to God excludes any kind of *shirk* or associating partners with God and withholding from God the devotion that only He deserves.[44]

And God knows best!

---

44. J. Hoover, *Ibn Taymiyya's Theodicy of Perpetual Optimism* (Leiden: Brill, 2007), p. 28.

28

Attributes of God

فَمِنْ سَبِيلِهِمْ فِي الْاِعْتِقَادِ: الْإِيمَانُ بِصِفَاتِ اللهِ تَعَالَى وَأَسْمَائِهِ
الَّتِي وَصَفَ بِهَا نَفْسَهُ وَسَمَّى بِهَا نَفْسَهُ فِي كِتَابِهِ وَتَنْزِيلِهِ أَوْ عَلَى
لِسَانِ رَسُولِهِ مِنْ غَيْرِ زِيَادَةٍ عَلَيْهَا وَلَا نَقْصٍ مِنْهَا وَلَا تَجَاوُزٍ لَهَا
وَلَا تَفْسِيرٍ لَهَا وَلَا تَأْوِيلٍ لَهَا بِمَا يُخَالِفُ ظَاهِرَهَا وَلَا تَشْبِيهِ
لَهَا بِصِفَاتِ الْمَخْلُوقِينَ؛ وَلَا سِمَاتِ الْمُحَدَثِينَ

One should know that the way of the Pious Predecessors
in belief is to have faith in the attributes of God, exalted
is He, and His names with which He has described
Himself and called Himself by in His Book and
revelation or which have come to us on the tongue of
His Messenger, without adding to them or subtracting
from them; without going beyond their obvious meaning,
or explaining them, or interpreting them figuratively in
a way that contradicts their apparent meaning; without
assimilating them with the attributes of created beings or
the features of the contingent.[45]

---

45. *Majmūʿ al-fatāwā*, 4: 5.

*T*he inquisition suffered by *Shaykh al-Islām* Ibn Taymiyyah over his theological writings has been well-documented in history. However, it is not always clear to people why he was persecuted to the extent that he was. Some have suggested that he was targeted for his unwillingness to acquiesce to Ashʿarite rationalism. The fact is, however, that traditionalists before Ibn Taymiyyah had promulgated Hanbalī creed in similar socio-political climes without fear of indictment. In Ibn Taymiyyah's case, the problem was configured in a rather unique way: he chose to defend a theological schema that, although appearing of Ḥanbalī inspiration, was, in fact, predicated on a populist vision which removed it from anything that could hitherto be considered 'orthodox'. It should be of little surprise that even many of his close friends felt very uneasy about Ibn Taymiyyah's radical new understanding, and over the course of his interactions with the authorities, felt the need to distance themselves from him.[46]

So what was it that rendered the theology of Ibn Taymiyyah so litigious? Firstly, he was a sharp-tongued polemicist whose vituperative criticism left few unscathed. Al-Dhahabī, whose biography of Ibn Taymiyyah has been translated by Caterina Bori, said, 'And there are people—whose malevolence and evil inclination are well known indeed—who insult him and charge him with unbelief.' They are either

---

46. Jackson, S.A., 'Ibn Taymiyyah on Trial in Damascus', *Journal of Semitic Studies* (1994), pp. 41-85, p. 40.

speculative theologians or *Ittiḥādī* Sufis or masters of dhikr or people he has offended and slandered in an exaggerated way, may God protect him from the evil in his soul [...] of the most authoritative speculative theologians and philosophers he says: "They do not know Islam and the revelation brought by the Prophet ﷺ" and about the spiritual states of many Sufi masters he says: 'They are satanic and possessed by their own selfish passions.'[47] This sort of rhetoric earnt Ibn Taymiyyah very few friends from within the scholarly classes. Secondly, he believed that he had developed a theological system that struck a fine balance between affirming a transcendent God without compromising or jeopardising the personal relationship between Him and His creatures—a median way in belief, or *wasaṭiyyah*. Certainly the outcome of his work was as complex as it was unique. Few understood, or wanted to understand, it, and many of these would take the opportunity to accuse him of anthropomorphism, one of the most heinous of theological crimes.

Ibn Taymiyyah was undeterred. He was driven by the view that mainstream theology alienated the common man: rationalist systems, which exert an upward pressure on the idea of the transcendence of God (*tanzīh*) threaten to place God beyond the conceptualisation of the ordinary worshipper; on

---

47. C. Bori, 'A New Source for the Biography of Ibn Taymiyya', *Bulletin for the Board of Oriental and African Studies*, 3 (2004), pp. 321-348.

the other hand, traditionalist schemas respond in a manner that offend the intellect. Both tendencies are inadequate, in Ibn Taymiyyah's mind, and so he developed a system which attempted to affirm the attributes of God as spoken about in the Qur'an and the Prophetic Tradition—thus protecting against figurative interpretations—while at the same time placing God beyond human likeness. And God knows best!

29

Leniency

لِلْعَالِمِ وَالْأَمِيرِ أَنْ ... يَعْفُوَ عَنِ الْأَمْرِ وَالنَّهْيِ بِمَا لَا يُمْكِنُ عِلْمُهُ وَعَمَلُهُ إِلَى وَقْتِ الْإِمْكَانِ

One shall with leniency abstain from commanding
and prohibiting things that it would not be possible
for people to know and implement until the time
when that becomes possible.[48]

I t is well-established in the Qur'an and Sunnah that a
Muslim must not only adhere to the highest ethical
and moral standards but must encourage others to
do so as well. God says, 'Let there arise out of you a
band of people inviting to all that is good, enjoining
what is right, and forbidding what is wrong: They
are the ones to attain felicity' (*al-Nisā'* 3: 104); 'You
are indeed the best community that has ever been
brought forth for [the good of] mankind: you enjoin

48. *Ibn Taymiyya: Against Extremisms*, p. 267.

the doing of what is right and forbid the doing of what is wrong, and you believe in God. Now if the followers of earlier revelation had attained to [this kind of] faith, it would have been for their own good; [but only few] among them are believers, while most of them are iniquitous' (*al-Nisā'* 3: 110). The Prophet ﷺ said, 'Whoever among you sees an evil action, let him change it with his hand; and if he cannot, then with his tongue; and if he cannot, then with his heart—and that is the weakest of faith' (Muslim). The over-arching doctrine is known as 'enjoining good and forbidding evil' (*al-amr bil-maʿrūf wal-nahy ʿanil-munkar*). Islam is unique in that it tasks every Muslim, scholar and layman, with this duty. The democratic aspect of this will no doubt strike a chord with many of us. Unfortunately, however, this can also be a recipe for disaster, as bigots, bullies, the arrogant and even some well-meaning folk police others under the remit of enjoining of good and forbidding evil. While the more experienced believer will probably be alert to the misuse of this, a new Muslim or someone not religiously literate could easily fall victim to misguided policing. *Shaykh al-Islām* Ibn Taymiyyah's words serve as an important intervention here. They are words directed towards the person who believes it is a duty on him to intervene in the lives of others. And lest such a person fear that they would be failing in their duty if they do not engage in *ḥisbah*, *Shaykh al-Islām* has the following reassuring words: 'To act in this way shall not signify approving prohibited things, nor abandoning commanding the obligatory things. Obligation and prohibition are indeed conditional on the possibility of knowledge and action. Now, we have hypothesized that this condition was not achieved. Ponder this fundamental principle!'[49] And God knows best!

---

49. *Ibn Taymiyya: Against Extremisms*, p. 268.

30

The Duty of Jihad

إِذَا هَجَمَ الْعَدُوُّ فَلَا يَبْقَى لِلْخِلَافِ وَجْهٌ فَإِنَّ دَفْعَ ضَرَرِهِمْ عَنِ
الدِّينِ وَالنَّفْسِ وَالْحُرْمَةِ وَاجِبٌ إِجْمَاعًا... وَأَمَّا قِتَالُ الدَّفْعِ
فَهُوَ أَشَدُّ أَنْوَاعِ دَفْعِ الصَّائِلِ عَنِ الْحُرْمَةِ وَالدِّينِ فَوَاجِبٌ
إِجْمَاعًا. فَالْعَدُوُّ الصَّائِلُ الَّذِي يُفْسِدُ الدِّينَ وَالدُّنْيَا لَا شَيْءَ
أَوْجَبَ بَعْدَ الْإِيمَانِ مِنْ دَفْعِهِ

When an enemy invades, then there is no scope for
debate: driving away the harm they pose to faith, life
and the inviolable becomes a religious duty according
to scholarly consensus. And since taking up arms is the
most robust way to repel an enemy, it itself becomes a
religious duty according to scholarly consensus. In fact,
after faith in God, there is no duty higher than driving
away an enemy intent on destroying everything, the
sacred and the profane.[50]

50. *Majmūʿ al-fatāwā*, 28: 223.

There can be no doubt that the taking up of arms is but one facet of jihad, and that the term jihad includes all forms of struggle, especially spiritual exertion and self-purification. This said there is no sensible reason why this point has to be laboured *ad nauseum* as it is in so many Muslim circles today, and there is absolutely no justification on the basis of the Qur'an, the Sunnah and the Muslim intellectual heritage for jihad as violent struggle, akin to the just war tradition in the West, to be written out of Islam. While it may be true that jihad has been hijacked by extremists who seek to justify their use of violence through religion, it is also clear that apologists who argue that violent jihad has no place in the modern world are merely capitulating to the extremists. And when they cite traditions in support of their agenda, such as the purported statement of the Prophet Muhammad ﷺ, 'We have returned from the lesser jihad to the greater jihad'—a statement supposedly made after the military expedition of Tabūk—they fail to realise the impotency of their attempt. Indeed *Shaykh al-Islām*, like all major Hadith masters, rejected the authenticity of this statement. According to him, 'This tradition has no basis and it has not been reported by anyone who has knowledge of the sayings and actions of the Prophet ﷺ. Undertaking jihad, in the form of a just war, against the unbelievers is from the greatest of actions, indeed it is the best action that a person could opt to perform. God says, "Not equal are those believers who sit (at home) and receive no hurt, and those who strive and fight (*mujāhidīn*) in the cause of God with their goods and their persons. God has granted a grade higher to those who strive and fight (*mujāhidīn*) with their goods and persons than to those who sit at home. Unto all has Allah promised good: But those who strive and fight (*mujāhidīn*) has He distinguished above those who sit at home by a special reward. Ranks specially bestowed by Him, and Forgiveness and Mercy. For God is Oft-forgiving, Most Merciful" (*al-Tawbah* 9: 95-96).'[51]

We have therefore to find a way to integrate the doctrine of jihad into the context of the modern age if we are to reclaim it from the extremists. The way to do so is to revive the jihad of classical Islam—the jihad which *Shaykh al-Islām* sets out in this statement. Jihad as understood in classical Islam—the Islam lived and taught by *Shaykh al-Islām*—is a form of military struggle embedded within state structures, authorised by a legitimate ruler, fought for the national interest and also for the love of one's nation. But there are aspects of the classical doctrine which would need to be stripped away, such as those which stem from its imperialistic context. There is no doubt that if jihad is understood as a struggle for Muslim hegemony, where Islam is privileged over other religions and the interests of Muslims over non-Muslims within the socio-political order, it will never be something that can be universally embraced, and the use of force to establish such hegemony will result in the association

---

51. *Majmūʿ al-fatāwā*, 11: 197.

of Islam with violence. However, if jihad is taken to mean the struggle to form and defend society as a whole—as is undertaken by the Armed Forces—it will be possible for the non-Muslim to participate alongside the Muslim in jihad, and for the Muslim to participate, in minority contexts, alongside the non-Muslim. Undoubtedly the goal would have to be unequivocally good, legitimising thereby the use of force. And God knows best!

31

Reason and Revelation

وَلَيْسَ فِي الْمَعْقُولِ مَا يُخَالِفُ الْمَنْقُولَ

There is nothing in the domain of reason that
conflicts with revelation.[52]

*T*he Qur'an, despite its complexity, has certainly
stood the test of time, remaining relevant even
through the great intellectual and civilisational shifts
which have characterized the last two centuries. In
fact, it has managed to remain relevant in a way
that perhaps no other sacred text has. How this has
been achieved is not the point here—more pertinent
is the fact that Ibn Taymiyyah was in no doubt
about the way the Qur'an stood up to the challenge
of reason back in the thirteenth century, and that
his confidence in it is still warranted seven hundred
years later. What he meant by revelation is clear—

---

52. *Majmūʿ al-fatāwā*, 12: 81.

the Qur'an and the soundly transmitted Sunnah. What is not so clear is what he meant by reason. According to *Shaykh al-Islām*, reason is equivalent to plain, sound rational thinking which emanates from *fiṭrah*, or innate nature. As long as the *fiṭrah* remains uncorrupted, reason can be trusted as a valid basis for knowledge. With regards to how revelation and reason may be understood as mutually reconcilable, a passage from Ibn Taymiyyah's letter to the Syrian prince, Abū l-Fidā', proves illustrative. The translation is by Jon Hoover:

> The [Pious Predecessors] and their followers knew that both revelational and rational proofs were true and that they entailed one another. Whoever gave rational and certain proofs [...] the complete inquiry due to them knew that they agreed with what the Messengers informed about and that they proved to them the necessity of believing the Messengers in what they informed about. Whoever gave revelational proofs [...] the understanding due them knew that God guided His servants in His Book to certain rational proofs by which are known the existence of the Creator, the subsistence of His attributes of perfection and His exoneration from imperfections and from anything being like Him in the attributes of perfection, and which prove His uniqueness, the uniqueness of His lordship, the uniqueness of His divinity, His power, His knowledge, His wisdom, His mercy, the truthfulness of His Messengers, the

obligation to obey them in what they obligate
and command, and believing them in what they
teach and inform about.[53]

As explained by Jon Hoover, in *Shaykh al-Islām*'s
system, revelation embodies true rationality. Once
one has the privilege of accessing revelation, it is
possible for them to see the correlation between it
and the truth known previously through reason. And
presaging Immanuel Kant by applying boundaries to
the scope of reason, *Shaykh al-Islām* says that only
revelation can lead to knowledge of the details of
theological matters, the angels, the Throne, Paradise,
the Fire and the details of what is commanded and
prohibited. Reason is only suitable for establishing the
existence of God, His attributes, and the obligation to
believe and obey what God has revealed through His
Messengers. And God knows best!

---

53. J. Hoover, *Ibn Taymiyya's Theodicy of Perpetual Optimism*
(Leiden Brill, 2007), p. 31.

32

The Shariah

لَفْظُ الشَّرْعِ فِي هَذَا الزَّمَانِ يُطْلَقُ عَلَى ثَلاَثَةِ مَعَانِ:
شَرْعٌ مُنَزَّلٌ وَشَرْعٌ مُتَأَوَّلٌ وَشَرْعٌ مُبَدَّلٌ

The term 'Shariah', embraces three meanings in our
time: revealed Shariah, interpreted Shariah, and
distorted Shariah.[54]

ne of the most important clarifications of *Shaykh
al-Islām* is surely that which he provided for the
term Shariah. For him there are three meanings in
common usage:

1. Revealed Shariah (*sharᶜ munazzal*), which
   embraces the Book (i.e. Qur'an) and the
   Sunnah. Everyone is obligated to live by
   this—anyone who claims that some people are
   excused from having to live by it is a disbeliever

---

54. *Majmūᶜ al-fatāwā*, 11: 199.

(*kafir*). God says: 'We sent aforetime our apostles with clear signs and sent down with them the Book and the Balance (of right and wrong), that men may stand forth in justice; and We sent down iron, in which is (material for) mighty war, as well as many benefits for mankind, that Allah may test who it is that will help, Unseen, Him and His apostles: For Allah is Full of Strength, Exalted in Might (and able to enforce His Will)' (*al-Ḥadīd*, 57: 25). God makes clear here that the Book and justice are inextricably bound—the Shariah is justice, and justice is Shariah. Therefore, whoever has judged with justice has judged by the Shariah.

2. Interpreted Shariah (*shar'mu'awwal*), which embraces those matters requiring intellectual inquiry (*ijtihād*) and about which the scholars have taken different views. To follow the opinion of any qualified jurisprudent (*mujtahid*) on an issue which one believes there to be a strong religious basis for is an acceptable course to take. *Shaykh al-Islām* warns us, however, that one should remain vigilant since there are times when interpretations conform to the Revealed Shariah and times when they do not. It is only the Prophet ﷺ, who is to be followed unconditionally.

3. Distorted Shariah (*shar'mubaddal*), which embraces fabricated Hadith, baseless interpretations, misguided deductions and prohibited

forms of traditionalism. It is ultimately injustice, and this is how it can be identified.

May God aid us in discerning the Revealed Shariah from the Distorted Shariah so that we might follow the way of justice in all of our affairs. And God knows best!

33

The Best Action

وَسُئِلَ: أَيُّمَا أَوْلَى مُعَالَجَةُ مَا يَكْرَهُ اللهُ مِنْ قَلْبِكَ مِثْلُ الْحَسَدِ
وَالْحِقْدِ وَالْغِلِّ وَالْكِبْرِ وَالرِّيَاءِ وَالسُّمْعَةِ وَرُؤْيَةِ الْأَعْمَالِ
وَقَسْوَةِ الْقَلْبِ وَغَيْرِ ذَلِكَ. مِمَّا يَخْتَصُّ بِالْقَلْبِ مِنْ دَرَنِهِ
وَخُبْثِهِ؟ أَوِ الِاشْتِغَالُ بِالْأَعْمَالِ الظَّاهِرَةِ: مِنَ الصَّلَاةِ
وَالصِّيَامِ وَأَنْوَاعِ الْقُرُبَاتِ مِنَ النَّوَافِلِ

The Shaykh was asked about which act is more worthy:
the act of the heart, such as curtailing envy, rancor,
scorn, arrogance, ostentation, etc., or the act of the
body, such as prayer, fasting and other devotions,
especially those which are optional.[55]

To this he replied, may God have mercy on him: 'There
are some actions which are indeed obligated (*wājib*)
upon man, yet that which is more incumbent (*awjab*)

55. *Majmūʿ al-fatāwā*, 11: 178-179.

is of greater merit and reward. God, the Exalted, has said through the words of His Prophet ﷺ: "My slave does not draw as close to Me as he does by performing that which I have obligated upon him," and then he said, 'And my slave continues to draw close to me through supererogatory acts, until I love him.' Now, the outward actions (aʿmāl ẓāhirah) are neither sound nor accepted unless they have been mediated by the action of the heart—indeed the heart is as a king and the limbs are its soldiers, such that when the king is corrupt, the soldiers also become corrupted. For this reason, the Prophet ﷺ said, "There lies within the body a piece of flesh. If it is sound, the whole body is sound; if it is corrupted, the whole body is corrupted." Similarly, the actions of the heart must surely affect the action of the body. There are instances when the more incumbent of two actions is the action of the inner (bāṭin), such as divesting oneself of envy and arrogance, which is more incumbent than performing supererogatory fasts. In other instances, the act of greater merit is that of the outward (ẓāhir), such as standing the night in prayer (qiyām al-layl), which is of greater merit than simply engaging in virtuous thoughts, such as ghibṭah (wishing for something someone else has without wishing for them to lose it). In fact, inner and outward acts support one another, so, for example, the prayer restrains from shameful and unjust deeds while at the same time bequeathing humility and having other great benefits. In fact, the prayer is the best of all actions when thought of like this, as is charity, and God knows best!'

34

The Way of the Salaf

فَمَنْ جَعَلَ طَرِيقَ أَحَدٍ مِنَ الْعُلَمَاءِ وَالْفُقَهَاءِ أَوْ طَرِيقَ

أَحَدٍ مِنَ الْعُبَّادِ وَالنُّسَّاكِ أَفْضَلَ مِنْ طَرِيقِ الصَّحَابَةِ

فَهُوَ مُخْطِئٌ ضَالٌّ مُبْتَدِعٌ

A mistaken and misguided innovator is he who
judges the method of a scholar or jurist, or the path
of an ascetic or hermit to be better than the way
of the Companions.[56]

Shaykh al-Islām Ibn Taymiyyah believed that every
Muslim ought to know that the best speech is the
revelation of God, the best guidance is that taught
by the Prophet Muḥammad ﷺ, and the best generation is that to which the Prophet ﷺ was sent.
Additionally, each Muslim ought to know that the
best path to God is that which the Prophet ﷺ and

---

56. *Majmūʿ al-fatāwā*, 11: 9.

his Companions were upon. This is what scholars consider to be the 'Salafism' of *Shaykh al-Islām*. It is a perspective which holds that the Companions, and indeed the early Muslims more generally, knew more about the religion and were more God-fearing than any other generation in the history of Islam. It is also a perspective which holds that the authentically reported interpretations of the early Muslims— the *salaf*—of the Qur'an are raised to the level of Prophetic traditions, and are to be given precedence over the interpretations of later generations. As explained by Rapoport and Ahmed,

> Although Ibn Taymiyyah's views represent a radical break from the theological traditions of his time, he does not see them as novel. Rather, he sees his role as that of retrieving the unity of reason and revelation advocated by the *salaf*, thereby peeling off the obscuring layers of interpretation added on in later centuries, often by well-meaning theologians and jurists. The closer one is to the original Prophetic message, the closer one gets to the truth.[57]

Furthermore, *Shaykh al-Islām*'s Salafism was iconoclastic inasmuch as it was critical of the binding authority of later interpretations (exegetical and legal) besides being reverential of the first community

---

57. Y. Rapoport and S. Ahmed, 'Introduction' in *Ibn Taymiyya and His Times* (Karachi: Oxford University Press, 2010), p. 11.

of Muslims. In this respect, his way can be read as a theology of liberation, one which freed the Muslims from the noose of every form of blind traditionalism. And God knows best!

Bibliography

Beron, M., *The Power of Labels* (Indiana: AuthorHouse, 2013).

Bori, C., *A New Source for the Biography of Ibn Taymiyya*, (Bulletin for the Board of Oriental and African Studies, Issue 3, 2004).

Brown, B., *The Gifts of Imperfection* (Minnesota: Hazelden, 2010).

Goldziher, I., *Introduction to Islamic Theology and Law* (New Jersey: Princeton University Press, 1981).

Hallaq, Wael, *Ibn Taymiyya on the Existence of God* (Acta Orientalia LII).

Hassan, Hassan, *The secret world of Isis training camps - ruled by sacred texts and the sword*, The Guardian, 25th Jan. 2015, https://www.theguardian.com/world/2015/jan/25/inside-isis-training-camps

Hoover, J., *Ibn Taymiyya's Theodicy of Perpetual Optimisim* (Leiden Brill, 2007).

Ibn Qayyim al-Jawziyyah, Shams al-Dīn, *Madārij al-sālikīn bayna manāzil iyyāka na'budu wa iyyāka nasta'īn* (Beirut: Dār al-kitāb al-'arabī, 1973).

———, *Al-Wābil al-ṣayyib fī al-kalim al-Ṭayyib* (Beirut: Dar al-kutub al-'ilmiyyah, 1998).

Ibn Taymiyyah, Taqī al-Dīn, *Iqtidā' al-ṣirāṭ al-mustaqīm, mukhālafat aṣhāb al-jahīm*, edited by 'Abd al-Hamīd al-Hindāwī (Beirut: Maktabat al-'aṣriyya, 2003).

———, *Majmū' al-fatāwā* (Beirut: Dār al-kutub al-'ilmiyyah, 2000).

———, *Diseases of the Hearts and Their Cures*, trans. Abū Rumaysah (Birmingham: Daar us-Sunnah, 2000).

Jackson, S.A., *Ibn Taymiyyah on Trial in Damascus* (Journal of Semitic Studies 1994).

Little, D., *The Historical and Historiographical Significance of the Detention of Ibn Taymiyya*, (International Journal of Middle East Studies (4) 1973).

Michot, Yahya, *Ibn Taymiyya: Against Extremisms* (Beirut: Al Bourak, 2012).

Rapoport, Y. and Ahmed, S., *Introduction in Ibn Taymiyya and His Times* (Karachi: Oxford University Press, 2010).

Shafak, Elif, *The forty rules of love* (Penguin Books, 2010).

Index